My Journey Through Turbulent Times of Life

AN AUTOBIOGRAPHY

Professor Martin Marial Takpiny

Copyright © Martin Marial Takpiny, 2017
ISBN: 978-0-9943631-7-6
Published by: Africa world books, Perth, Australia
Edited by Cheryl Bettridge AE and Catherine Schwerin
All rights reserved
No parts of this book may be reproduced or transmitted in any form or by any means, graphic, electronic, or mechanical, including photocopying, recording, taping or by any information storage retrieval system, without permission in writing from the author.
Design and typesetting of text: All In One Book Design
Cover design: Dut Atem, atemdesign.com

Contents

Introduction, 5

Key to standard and local abbreviations, 21

Chapter One   The Beneficiaries, 23

Chapter Two   Village Life, 27

Chapter Three   Numeracy and Literacy in Exemplary School, 37

Chapter Four   Career, 43

Chapter Five   Politics, 53

Chapter Six   Academic Life, 60

Chapter Seven   A Refugee in East Africa, 73

Chapter Eight   Immigration to the Land of the Kangaroo, 88

Epilogue, 99

References, 105

Acknowledgements, 107

Introduction

The author of this life story, Martin Marial Takpiny, requires little introduction to many South Sudanese readers. Now a retired senior citizen in Australia as well of his native South Sudan, he was born in 1940 to a Dinka chiefly family in the former Yirol District of Southern Sudan. From his rural roots, he later rose to become a school teacher, a legislator, provincial commissioner – with powers similar to those held by a South Sudanese state governor or premier in Australia – twice a political detainee under Sudan's two dictatorial regimes in the late 1970s through to the 1980s and 1990s. Marial's other notable experience include having been a university dean; and finally, an internally displaced person, together with his family.

The author has seen it all: bad and good days, glory and humiliation, pain and happiness, at different times and in different places during his many years as a public servant. This was an era characterised by turbulence caused by Sudan's brutal and long civil wars of 1955–1972 (Anya Nya), 1975-1983 (Anya Nya Two) and 1983–2005 (SPLM/SPLA). The three armed conflicts pitted the insurgents from what is today the independent state of South Sudan against the various governments that came and went in Khartoum, and which they accused of running a system of rule based on exclusion and discrimination of other citizens on racial and religious grounds.

The writer and the readers of this book should consider themselves lucky. Were he to delay for another three more years in committing to paper his life story, the chances are that his experiences would have continued to reside in his memory, not in this form. The draft that became the book was written not long before he partially lost his eyesight as a result of diabetes. This means, unfortunately, he will not able to see the colours in which the book appears or the lines that he wrote, the shape and size of this book, or this Introduction. At any rate, he will be happy, as he was, like many authors, not writing for himself but for the younger and future generations of fellow South Sudanese at home and around the world.

With the publication of this book, Prof Martin Marial Takpiny has practically joined the rank of the very few South Sudanese public figures who understand and appreciate the importance of documenting their experiences – personal and public – as a resource to be shared. Among most of his South Sudanese peers, the author is likely to provoke in them a sense of vicarious participation in the narratives and events retold here, or to be temporarily seized by a twinge of nostalgia or sadness, as individual cases may dictate. As for the younger generation and posterity or for readers from different cultural or ethnic backgrounds, some of the episodes are likely to provide them with a first-hand "report" on the distant past from an eyewitness. Past Dinka world of belief systems and values to which he introduces the reader at the beginning, is a case in point.

This is not a matter of conjecture; in a previous conversation with me, the author made it clear that he was motivated to write his reminiscences to record for posterity some aspects of the past society he belonged to. These recollections too, form a kind of his own legacy that will shed some light on the world that is hardly recognisable today. Since many of the South Sudanese major actors have not written about their lives and roles in the events, some tumultuous and historic – much of our recent history expected from participants and witnesses has, regrettably, been lost. That this is happening in a society with a sizeable number of literate members of the ruling elites is unfortunate. Late Dr William Kon Bior, a lawyer and one of his country's prominent intellectuals, attributed this phenomenon to what he called "oral society syndrome". To him, the culprit responsible for the phenomenon is lack of literacy but because he believed many members of South Sudanese educated class prefer spoken communication to its written form. The consequence of this culture is that knowledge of public affairs is being passed on by word of mouth which gets distorted along the way. Seen from that angle, this book is a welcomed contribution to the huge amount of information that could be recalled from memory.

By choosing to write his life story, and being one of the South Sudanese public figures who have made some visible and indelible marks on their society, Martin Marial Takpiny is in the lead in doing what only a few members of his generation and peers have done: picking and documenting, from a personal viewpoint, some aspects of South Sudan's past political, cultural and social silhouette. When I describe the author as being one of the few among former senior public servants to publish their memoirs, I am alluding to those who have gone without writing personal stories. They are many but only a few are named here. Notable "absentees" include Joseph Oduho (a former school teacher like Marial and a founding member of the first armed resistance), William Deng

Nhial, Aggrey Jaden Lako, Daniel Jumi Tongun, former civil servant and one of the participants in the 1955 Torit mutiny (Uncle Jumi, as he was popularly known to many South Sudanese, held another record of a kind: longevity which took him beyond a 100-year watershed).

There were other pioneers, mostly past political party leaders and government ministers before Sudan's independence from Britain in 1956, whose life stories would have made a significant contribution to the understanding of the times and what was happening then. Unfortunately, what they did, stood for or said, is communicated by living contemporaries or being passed on from generation to generation, all orally, subjecting the authenticity of their testimonies and roles each played, to inevitable distortion, deliberate or otherwise. Scepticisms arising out of such accounts can be justified.

The names (of the 1950s-1960s politicians) which easily come to mind, not necessarily in that order, include politicians such as Buth Diu, Fr Saturnino Lohure, Luigi Adwok Bong (the first and the only citizen from Southern Sudan to have been a ceremonial head of the Sudanese State), Alfred Barjok, Bullen Alier de Bior, Benjamin Lwoki, Gordon Apeec Ayom, Ferdinand Adiang, Ezboni Mondiri Gwanza, Elijah A. Mayom, Gordon Muortat Mayen, Parmena Bul Koch, Clement Gutia Mboro, Samuel Abu John Kabash, Peter Gatkuoth Gual, Philip Obang. It is a virtually an inexhaustible list.

One of outstanding South Sudanese personalities whose memoirs are likely to be published posthumously is Hilary Logali. A fellow journalist has intimated to me that Hilary who was an undisputed intellectual, has left a manuscript of his autobiography.

~

The author is being modest when he states at the onset "I haven't done something spectacular in life to let somebody write about me". As a public figure or any other human being for that matter, Martin Marial Takpiny, as far as public knowledge is concerned, has not been involved in any hair-raising exploits or scandalous conducts or omissions that normally attract media headlines. As a loving husband, father of adult children, a doting grandfather and a human being above all, his life, similar to that led by other respectable family men and women, falls into the category of the expected: living within the confines of the straight and the narrow. That kind of life can be described as boringly normal. Not surprisingly, in the world where the unconventional, the outrageous or the prurient – which fuel gossips and whispered scandals involving society's high and mighty – the accepted and expected code of conduct hardly attracts those hungry for sensationalism. On the other plane, self-appointed hagiographers would only take interest – also with an eye on recompense in one form or another – if the subject happens to wield enormous amount of power, wealth or both.

However, it should not be forgotten that writing and reading are not all about entertainment; most people read primarily to be informed about some serious matters or less exciting events that are important to an understanding of past or current issues. Any form of knowledge which is derived from the experiences of other people, like some of the episodes in this book, becomes an additional contribution to an understanding of contemporary history. This book contains bits of information which throw light on the intelligentsia from South Sudan and their politics. One of these is the revelation by the author that the former governor of Bahr el Ghazal State, Ali Tamim Fartak was planning to harm him. The two men were once members of Southern Front, a political party that strongly advocated for the rights of the people of Southern Sudan. The governor, he says, targeted him for possible physical elimination. That Marial Takpiny had to flee Wau for the countryside is an indication that the threat to his life was real. The incident also says a lot about what political opportunism does to some people: pursuit, acquisition and maintenance of power at all costs.

Marial's life story begins with a brief outline of the traditional Dinka society of his boyhood during the 1940s. Each of these episodes takes the reader to the little known and less documented – except by European anthropologists – ways the rural people lived at the time and the belief system and practices that were dominant then.

Although the author does not claim to be writing a social history of his people, some of the events he has narrated here introduce the reader, especially from the younger generation and non-South Sudanese backgrounds, to what life was like before formal education and what some people would describe as modernity, had seeped into African societies anchored on traditional belief systems and practices which governed most aspects of people's lives through millennia.

Those were the times, for instance, when confronted with misfortunes, illness or death, most rural population would attribute their causes to angry spirits or an act by a malevolent person. Members of the younger generation today are likely to react "Oh, those superstitious ancients!", and probably with a tinge of embarrassment in their voices. Nevertheless, passing value judgement – condemnation or approval – on such beliefs and practices of past era misses a point: the writer is simply telling some of those customs as they were; he is giving – as a keen observer – an honest picture of the way people lived.

The stories in themselves and their telling are indifferent. And much of that kind of knowledge is fading. In a way the writer is like a guard taking a visitor into a museum. Were he to gloss over the warts and all, a true picture of what really obtained would have been obscured. The result of that would have been an airbrushed account of the people and their culture.

The fact that the author has resisted the temptation to present a rosy portrait of his society as it was during his early years, marks him out for honesty. We should be grateful that someone who is an eyewitness is recalling and recording images from the past for others who did not have the chance to personally experience those things. What is being given to a younger reader is a piece of information about the past that is no longer there. The writer is not asking anyone to approve or condemn how people then lived in villages of the territory that is now South Sudan. In recalling those events and ethos, Martin Marial Takpiny, the septuagenarian, is actually saying: this is how people lived in their world and time.

Whether this observation is correct or not, few among the younger generation are aware of that fact. This is an area which has suffered neglect: there are very few documented resources, either as subjects of academic research or memoirs. This, I think, justifies the publication of this life story. The author's social mobility from a Dinka cattle herder and as a son of traditional chief who rose to become a legislator, a provincial commissioner and finally a university professor before retiring, is story of personal achievement meriting a book of this type. This story is likely to inspire many young people, especially from Africa in general and South Sudan in particular.

Part of this account takes the reader to the past of an African setting in which there are many customs, some based on time-honoured practices and beliefs such as the power of traditional healers, the exercise and transfer of political power within the clan, the institution of polygyny, to name some of the prominent features of a society governed by traditions. One going through the pages of these recollections is in a similar situation as a person being shown a film presenting the life of a community of several decades ago and whose ways of life have changed radically in the intervening time.

Despite being a discerning educationist and a caring father and grandfather, Prof Marial Takpiny is uncomfortable and impatient with what he sees as an erosion of social norms that governed the society of his boyhood and youth. In particular, he decries the fact that young people are no longer being taught the lineage system. In the past, Dinka children were trained to know by heart their family trees and at puberty had to make sure that they also knew the lineage of any other young person especially from the opposite sex. The idea behind this is that Dinka marriage customs prescribe some of the most rigid taboos in the world; any remotest blood-relationship would automatically preclude marriage or sexual intimacy between persons who could be considered related even if their ancestors were many generations apart.

In Chapter One of this book, the writer tells how people lived then and how the kinship network bound individual members to the family and families to families and the entire clan. And he was the beneficiary of that "dynastic" system. Following the death of his father, his uncle, Dhieu Malual, became chief. It was Chief Dhieu who took young Marial, his nephew, to school. Relatives had, and are still expected today, to take moral responsibility to work for the welfare of their kin.

Being among the few who went to school in the late 1940s, Marial was sent to Tonj Primary School, very far from home. The school was a world of formal education, from book learning which in those days, made the teacher as the fountain of knowledge which he fed to somewhat passive pupils; interactive education had not been conceived, let alone introduced. Physical education especially sports played a role as was observance of strict discipline whose violation meant severe corporeal punishment.

Side by side with the acquisition of book knowledge, the pupils continued to live more or less the same way they had been brought up in the village and cattle camp. Each boy was accompanied by a milking cow to provide him with milk. The author tells us that pupils rarely wore clothes and so forth.

Prior to his enrolment in elementary school, Marial recalls it was widely believed that the conduct of some among the boys who had completed or left primary school halfway and returned home did not make formal education and its outcome attractive to the community. Marial says that some of those early school leavers became a disappointment to society, adding that the bad apples among those young men gave the traditional society the perception that book learning only produced failures and "idlers and drunkards". But with Marial and his peers doing well at school and conducting themselves responsibly, the way soon began to open for mass education.

Although modest at the beginning, the school was a key that was going to open the world of opportunities to successful students. Marial was one of them. After obtaining his Seondary School Certificate, Martin Marial Takpiny, through failure in communication, missed being taken on a government scholarship to study abroad, so he ended up as a school teacher at Bussere Intermediate School, not far from Wau, the capital of his home province of Bahr el Ghazal. At Bussere, one of his students happened to be the man who was going to make history and one of the recognisable African leaders of the late

20th century and early 21st century: John Garang. Marial's former student went on to become leader of the Sudan People's Liberation Movement, SPLM, and its military component, the Sudan People's Liberation Army, the SPLA, an insurgency organisation that waged military and political struggle against the central government of Sudan. The rebellion was waged under the banner of justice, equality and democracy for the majority of the Sudanese people. Before dying in a helicopter crash in 2005, Garang was the first vice-president of Sudan and head the self-governing Southern Sudan.

Determined to go for further studies, Marial went to the American University of Beirut in Lebanon in the late 1960s where he received both bachelor and master degrees in education. On return to Sudan Martin Marial Takpiny taught in secondary school and teachers' training institute before his promotion to head planning unit at the ministry education headquarters in Juba in the 1970s. He also served as deputy headmaster of Rumbek Secondary School, his alma mater.

Whether as a student or a school teacher or a university lecturer, Marial, like most members of his generation, went through two devastating civil wars, resulting in deaths estimated at 2.5 million South Sudanese, civil strife and social dislocation within Southern Sudan. The armed conflict was intermittent, lasting over half a century of political and social turbulence, hence the tittle of the book. The conflict owed its origins to the time when a company of soldiers from the South who were stationed at Torit garrison in Equatoria Province mutinied on 18 August 1955 against their Northern officers. What later became known officially as disturbances spread like wildfire to the rest of Southern Sudan. Education was one of the first casualties as all the schools in the region were closed for a complete academic year; some schools such as Rumbek

Secondary where Marial was in the final year were relocated to Northern Sudan.

The restive region became a highly politicised society, with regular politically motivated students strikes taking place from time to time, resulting in frequent closures.

The Addis Ababa Agreement of 1972 between the Government of Sudan and the rebels of the Southern Sudan Liberation Movement, SSLM, created executive and legislative organs for the region. In 1978, Marial Takpiny contested election to the Regional Assembly and won. After a short stint as a backbencher, the former teacher was appointed commissioner of Lakes Province. Although Sudan as a whole was a one party state at the time, political parties operated, albeit unofficially, in the Southern region. Marial, the commissioner, belonged to Southern Front, a political party which was a rival to Sudan African National Union, Sanu. Joseph Lagu who succeeded Abel Alier of Southern Front, was Sanu's candidate when he won the HEC presidency in 1978. Marial's removal as commissioner was due to a power struggle between the two parties. His replacement in the post had his own problems which he blamed on his predecessor. Former commissioner Martin Marial Takpiny was arrested and detained at the orders of his successor. The former provincial administrator says his humiliation was greatest when he was placed in a cell which he had to share with common criminals in a jailhouse he used to inspect when he held authority. But that was just the beginning of hard times ahead.

After the outbreak of the conflict of the second civil war, incidentally led by Dr John Garang, Marial's former student, he had joined the staff of the newly created University of Juba where he became a lecturer at the department of education. In Juba, and later when the university was transferred to

Khartoum the capital because of the armed conflict in the South, Marial was falsely charged with being a secret member of the rebel movement and was placed under detention. Even after his release he remained under the watchful eyes of the agents of the repressive state security organ.

In Khartoum, students and other young men were forcibly recruited into the army of the Islamist regime which had come to power through a military coup in 1989. The recruits were given crash military training before they were sent to the theatre of war in the South. Fearing that his only son, Takpiny, and who was a student in Khartoum, would be forcibly recruited to fight against his own people, Marial secretly sent him out of the country, to Syria first under the pretext that the youth was going to study in the Levant. Takpiny junior later found his way to Canada as a refugee. Despite the happy ending for the son, his father continued to be trailed by security operatives who suspected him of being a member of an alleged rebels' fifth column.

With the opening of the University of Bahr el Ghazal in Wau back in Southern Sudan, Marial was promoted to the rank of associate professor and made dean of College of Education of the new university. The appointment was not a favour but a way of sending him to the South which was a war zone and where government security operatives were a law unto themselves. The governor of the state in which the university was located was one Ali Tamim Fartak. Ali Tamim and Marial were once members of the defunct Southern Front party which in the 1970s made him the first ever Muslim cabinet minister in the overwhelmingly Christian Southern Sudan.

Since the coming to power of the Muslim fundamentalist oriented government, Ali Tamim Fartak had become more radical than the top leadership of the ruling National Islamic

Front. Tamim's appointment as governor was to give him a free hand to implement strict sharia or Islamic law and when necessary help in conversion of the state citizenry. The other mission of the governor was to combat what the government in Khartoum perceived as the influence of the SPLA rebels in the south of the country. The police state that Sudan had become allowed security agents to poke their noses into matters such as administrative, and even academic affairs of public institutions such as universities or entertainment organisations. In the absence of the university's vice chancellor, the security agent at the institution of higher learning had the guts to demand that he should become acting vice chancellor. Objection to the interference of security in affairs of the university was an invitation to problems for the academics who were not affiliated to the ideology of the regime.

During one of his public rallies in Wau, Governor Ali Tamim Fartak referred to Prof Marial Takpiny – by name – as one of the dangerous citizens in town, an allegation that gave the security elements the right to go after him; monitoring his daily movements and contacts he made. After realising that his life was in danger, Marial and his wife decided that it was time for them – the whole family – to sneak out of the beleaguered city. One by one, the family members left Wau at night. Relieved that they had escaped with their skins, the family regrouped and embarked on a long trek into the interior that was under the control of the SPLM/A.

To his pleasant surprise, the first military outpost the exhausted family reached was under the command of an officer who was Marial's former student. Commander Ajongo Mawut gave his former teacher a VIP reception that included organising a feast for the family. The rebel officer sent the news of the safe arrival of Marial and family to his superior commander and Marial's former student, John Garang. The SPLM/A leader made the arrival of the professor a news item which was sent to all the rebels' units.

Rumbek town has a special meaning for Prof Marial Takpiny. It was there where he, as a pupil, received part of his primary education, and later high school. Rumbek Secondary was the first and only of its kind in Southern Sudan. Years afterwards, Marial returned as a teacher and deputy headmaster, and by that time, a happily married young man. After going into politics, Rumbek was his headquarters of Lakes Province where he ran an area the size of some independent African countries and with a population of about a million inhabitants. One of his responsibilities was the provision of security to largely pastoral communities who often fight each other to death over water and grazing lands.

At Rumbek he tasted humiliation when he was accused by his political rival of causing trouble. For that the former provincial commissioner was confined to a prison where he had previously visited lawbreakers. At the time he was in Rumbek in the late 1990s, the town had suffered as a result of a 21-year civil war which had destroyed nearly all the buildings, including the province headquarters, Rumbek Secondary School, among others. It was a desolate place to be for someone who had once seen the town's glory and of which he was part of. And his pride, too. He and his family, like all the residents of the newly liberated town, had to sleep in the open, exposed to the elements.

Although the town was now under the resource-strapped rebels, it was a vital link to the outside world. Marial and family were then able to fly out to Nairobi, the capital of Kenya, where he got a job, almost on arrival, as an educational consultant to an indigenous church organisation, the

New Sudan Council of Churches, NSSCC. From Kenya the family later moved to Uganda where the children went to school. It was in that country where he was able to find the chance for resettlement with his family in Australia. His primary objective for such a decision was to find educational opportunities for his six daughters.

Teachers in most of the developing world, especially in the Arab and African cultures, are held in reverence by society in general as well as by their students. In Sudan teachers are referred to reverentially as Ustaz or Ma'lim. In Kiswahili, the teacher is *mwalimu*. Julius Nyerere, the founding father of Tanzanian nation who was a school teacher before going into politics, was universally known by the honorific of Mwalimu throughout his life, a title he preferred to "His Excellency" or President.

For decades Martin Marial Takpiny taught in several secondary schools of South Sudan and later became a lecturer at the faculty of education of the University of Juba. Towards the close of the last century, he became associate professor and founding dean of the new University of Bahr el Ghazal. Between the two civil wars, Martin Marial entered politics during which time he was elected to the People's Regional Assembly, the legislature of the then self-governing Southern Sudan. He served briefly as commissioner of his Lakes home province.

As a school teacher and later university lecturer, Martin Marial Takpiny has taught many students, some of them who are now among South Sudan's ruling elites- leaders in politics, military, business, academia, among others. His former students include Dr John Garang, the former leader of the SPLM/A, James Wani Igga, the current vice president of South Sudan, among other prominent public figures.

As a person who has educated several generations of his compatriots, the emeritus professor can look back with justified pride for his contribution to his nation and humanity.

This book is a welcomed contribution to the understanding of social and political evolution of the society of South Sudan, the world's youngest and struggling nation.

© Atem Yaak Atem 2017
Gosford, New South Wales, Australia

Key to Standard and Local Abbreviations

Esq	Esquire – Title of authority used during colonial rule.
HEC	High Executive Council, the council of minister of the self-governing Southern Region of Sudan as defined by the Addis Ababa Agreement of 1972.
IOM	International Organisation for Migration.
IDP	Internally displaced person.
JCSSS	Juba Commercial Senior Secondary School (previously Juba Commercial Secondary but from the 1970s changed, like all the schools in Sudan of the time, to Juba Commercial Senior Secondary School).
JTC	Juba Training Centre.
LRA	Lord's Resistance Army.
NCP	National Congress Party.
NIF	National Islamic Front.
NSCC	New Sudan Council of Churches.
NGO	Non-government organisation.
RSSS	Rumbek Senior Secondary School (previously Rumbek Secondary, changed to Rumbek Senior Secondary School after the introduction of "Education Ladder in early 1970s).
SANU	Sudan African National Union, one of the political parties speaking for Southern Sudan during the 1960s.
SIL	Summer Institute of Linguistics.
SCC	Sudan Council of Churches.
SPLM/A	Sudan People's Liberation Movement Army.

Southern Sudan	The name given to the southern third of the country which was given self-rule in 1972 by the Addis Ababa Agreement. It was sometimes referred to as Southern Region. The Comprehensive Peace Agreement, CPA, of 2005, established and interim administration, pending the holding of referendum to decide on unity or secession, called Government of Southern Sudan or GoSS.
South Sudan	After the people of the former Southern Sudan voted in 2011 for secession from Sudan, the region gained independence on 9 July 2011 and became South Sudan. Some people write it Republic of South Sudan, RSS.
TAFE	Technical and Further Education.
Toch	Dinka and Nuer word for swamp, Anglicised as toich.

Chapter One

The Beneficiaries

One of the main activities among youth in the evening is story telling. It is quite entertaining to both young and old. Stories from elders are educative and range from fear of indiscipline, lying or bravery instilled into the minds of the youth. No other sources of these stories are found. It's indicative that a community is illiterate when no books of traditions are recorded. No literate persons put the culture of the people in print in the form of fairy tales, old folks' tales, whether fiction or real. The community depends on oral tales for history.

A few years ago some books appeared on the market, generally on the Jiëëng (Dinka) and nearly all of them written by non-Dinka authors. The community where I come from is basically illiterate and the educated persons from my immediate section are very few. There's a great need for us, the few literate, to record our culture. Our society is in a transitional period socially, educationally, politically and economically. The period needs considerable documentation of positives and taboos for coming generations. Carefully and slowly, oral history needs to be replaced by well researched documentaries. It's a start to make journals to be kept at family and community levels.

For instance, the Dinka people are keen to know of kinship to avoid marriage or sexual intercourse of related persons. They know marriage between blood relatives is regarded as taboo by the culture. Consequently, children need to know their family tree back to their great, great, great grandparents. The situation is, there are no knowledgeable elders to orient the youth to family genealogy because the elders died in civil war and of illnesses. If each family keeps an entry of essential facts, it's better, yet the level of illiteracy is still very high.

I am alerting my generation to take note of this writing. The war made us disperse like birds of the air and the youth lost their sense of kinship, which is a pillar of Dinka culture. The beneficiaries of this book are to be my colleagues in my section, clan and others at large. It's intended for youth transition. The Dinka culture forbids marriage of kin, such as cousins marrying cousins or nieces, as this is incest.

The youths in the diaspora hardly know their fiancés, just the first or second name of the fiancé and not the names of their parents. For instance, a boy may know his fiancée (future wife) as Ann Aguot Wol and she only knows the boy as Costa William Dut and no more. It's not known whether the pair share blood relationships. Through genealogy it could be determined by elders in order to avoid unsuitable marriages.

According to Dinka culture the lineage of two families is to be thoroughly dissected to discover undesirable characteristics. Once there is a doubt the marriage is given up quietly at an early stage.

Early on, settlement was by a clan in a village. The inhabitants were related and as the children became adolescents, they were fully aware of connections among the village inhabitants. What helps the adolescents is the initiation process which introduces them to adulthood. The ritual conducted automatically allows the adolescents to behave as adults. The initiation 'pëlräk', which literally means "giving up milking cows", as known in the Ciec section, forbids the adolescent males from the adolescence crisis as known worldwide. 'Pëlräk' does the trick with the Ciec section, completing the transition from boyhood to manhood.

With a girl, the first menstruation brings respect to her and the new status of womanhood. Rituals and procedures are performed to let everybody know the girl has become of age, to be accorded recognition and to adopt a code of behaviour expected of her. The girls are constantly warned to follow the good behaviour expected of them and that menstruation means they will be ready for marriage soon.

The children are told frequently not to quarrel among themselves because they are related, as fighting was justified only to prepare for aggression coming from outside the clan.

The two wars in the South (1955–1972 and 1983–2005) ravaged the social network of the communities. There was migration to camps within the South and immigration to far lands never heard of by our parents. Under these conditions important aspects of the Dinka culture were being lost such as the traditions supposed to be preserved by parents who are themselves not well informed. A very large number of people become parents during and between the two wars and were not aware of what facts of the culture needed to be preserved or salvaged. It is beyond the scope of this book to indicate what parts of our culture need to be revived. The author feels that the genealogy of a family should be opened up to the youths wherever the parents reside.

We need to teach family genealogy to children in order for them to know who is their kin and avoid incest, as it is prohibited by the Dinka norms. For instance, in simple terms my family tree runs paternally like this: Takpiny, Marial, Takpiny,

Malual, Apar, Ayiec, Ater, Rou, Acot, Ngarbek, Putdo, Lietic, Erjok, Kuot, Monybai, Rupieu. Pictorially, it looks more impressive like this:

- 1 Takpiny
- 2 Marial
- 3 Takpiny
- 4 Malual
- 5 Apar
- 6 Ayiec
- 7 Ater
- 8 Rou
- 9 Acot
- 10 Ngarbek
- 11 Putdo
- 12 Lietic
- 13 Erjok
- 14 Kuot
- 15 Monybai
- 16 Rupieu

This forms sixteen generations, and brothers, sisters, siblings, uncles, aunts, cousins, nieces, nephews and grandparents inserted as branches merge with branches of other family trees to become a huge tree, which is a whole community.

A typical family tree looks like a big mature banyan tree (Ficus benglalensis) whose branches produce aerial roots that become trunks. The genealogy is one of the cornerstones of our traditions. Let it be noted that I am not attempting to write the anthropology of a society.

Chapter Two

Village Life

Parial or Parial Gok is a village about five miles north of Yirol town. There are many villages around it, all settlements on ironstone ground to avoid flooding during the rainy season. Rainwater goes to the Toch and flows towards the Sudd region. Parial is near a river which has many names. It is Mundri River southwards from the Yirol area, Payiei or Warthii in the middle and Moc River at the border of the Nuer territory on its way to the Sudd. When pools and wells dry up during the dry season, people and cattle move to it.

Parial village was the administrative seat of Paramount Chief Takpiny Malual Apar. He was a paramount chief of the Yirol sub-district, the centre of government of the district of the three tribes of Aliap, Atuot and Ciec. The British colonial administration awarded Chief Takpiny the first class belt of honour in recognition of his keen, fair and just judgement in tribal courts and disputes settlement. Paramount Chief Takpiny Malual Apar was illiterate, as was the whole population of the sub district. Literacy was a phenomenon not yet introduced by white man, the magicians who could see actions and words on a piece of paper, a widespread belief then held by the natives of the land.

To clear up misunderstandings by then, in the colonial archives of the Lakes district in Rumbek, Takpiny was written as Takpiny Aluker Apar. He became known as Takpiny Aluker in Rumbek, Bor, Tonj, Gogrial and Aweil areas where he conducted cases. The writer is well informed of the family lineage and Kooc tradition corrected the name to Takpiny Malual, to be explained in Chapter Three.

Yali, near Parial, was a local market where one could buy salt, beads and cloth needed by the girls. The women were content with wearing the skins of goats and sheep as a form of skirt. The men wore few clothes, especially the heads of the sections or gol (clan) leaders. The gol leaders met the assistant district commissioner, ADC, at times of poll tax collection and during court sessions.

It has been rationalised that climate contributes to the state of affairs of people being naked in the whole area. The culture of that allowed young men and children to go about unclothed in the past was not really to be blamed. The climate is neither cold nor hot, but there is high humidity in the atmosphere which is believed to have contributed to this state of affairs. However, necessity bade females to wear leather aprons instead of cloth skirts while young men openly took pride in wearing nothing. Some even used this to show off how well made their bodies were. If a young man were to wear a cloth, he could be ridiculed and nobody would step up to discourage it. The change was slow to come as is the case with other forms of social change.

The people of Parial like others in Southern Sudan in that day were subsistence cultivators or farmers. Traditional tools were used to cultivate sorghum, millet, groundnuts, beans and a few vegetables. The produce was mainly for subsistence and not for commercial purposes.

The meagre cultivation products were supplemented by cattle milk, especially in the dry season when many people would be in the camps at the edges of the swamps of the Sudd, where there's a lot of fish. Though only a few people would get a little of that lot of fish, if it could be fished on a large scale and shared more would benefit. The idea of sharing is predominant in the Dinka culture.

The year has two distinct times of dry and rainy seasons. In the dry season, the people would go to the toch (swampy land) with cattle and would depend on milk and little fish. There would be no normal work done whatsoever through the time spent in the camps. Both young and old would just sit under temporary sheds singing songs or conversing day in and day out. There would be occasional dancing. In short, a culture of idleness developed and was gradually passed on and became normal.

The situation was different in the rainy season. A small number would cultivate, and it was mainly women who were expected to carry out the process of cultivation. Men would help the women with cultivation, while the male youth would be in the camps or travel from village to village, almost aimlessly. The youths were more concerned with dancing and getting fat in the camps. After the fattening period there would again be a lot of dancing and singing.

The same few persons who cultivated the land during the previous rainy season would weed crops and it was not long before it was time to start harvesting. More young men would come to the villages to help in eating from the plentiful new yields, and a quarter of what had been harvested was consumed at that time.

In essence, the responsibility of cultivation is that of the elders, with no way to reverse that established pattern. Very few persons help the elders with cultivation. No doubt if everybody got involved in cultivation there would be a surplus produce for trade.

It is well known that the cow is the livelihood of the Dinka people. It gives milk in the morning and evening. Life is based on the cow and if anything, or anyone tries to take it away, the owner protects it to death. The cow encourages dependency on it and discourages people from working. There's no need to toil when a cow provides something you can comfortably survive on. It makes people hang on to it as a source of life. Survival is very easy. A person finds ways and means to have more cattle. This is what leads many people to work in towns to buy cattle. The dependency on cattle in turn develops complacency towards the cattle to the point that it sometimes encourages raiding. For example, cattle raiding is endemic in the Lakes State, especially in Yirol County, where many people lost their lives, more than when the South fought the central government controlled by the North.

After outlining general life in Parial, let an event be explored. It is an occurrence that gives substance to this writing. One rainy season three ladies were pregnant. Nothing abnormal about that, but two delivered and their immediate families rejoiced. The third was expecting to follow her colleagues in a matter of days. Expectations developed into anxiety for the expecting lady. The traditional midwife and other elderly women comforted her that it was normal.

In the modern world, it would be a matter of minutes to know whether something may be wrong. In Parial or Yirol town of the time in question there was nothing to be done. One day after midnight, the lady went into labour. The traditional midwife was at hand with her necessary materials. The relatives in the house awoke and unease prevailed. After midnight, to the surprise of everyone in the house, the lady gave birth with ease.

Suddenly, anxiety merged into euphoria, extreme happiness about the ease with which the traditional midwife had delivered the child and that the baby was a boy. The boy was the firstborn son of the man, so the persons present in the hut were full of jubilation. The news of the arrival of a baby boy flashed to the father in his compound two hundred metres from the hut of the mother. The father visited the homestead with a few other people, the well-wishers. Everybody felt elated and news spread to the homesteads of relatives.

The man didn't have a male child until now and the time came for him to remember his pride bull among the bride cattle wealth. He now bore an heir to his traditional position. A name for the newborn son should not be an issue as it should follow the custom of giving a son the name of an outstanding bull among the bride cattle wealth, or vice versa for a girl.

The man announced to relatives and well-wishers seated around him that the baby boy's name would be Marial. It was applauded because the name fitted. His pride Marial bull was known by his colleagues. That was Marial Takpiny Malual. The boy became Christian, christened as Martin Marial Takpiny, he was the first to be educated and Christian in the family of Apar. The paramount chief Takpiny Malual Apar was celebrating the birth of his first male child to be heir of his position.

According to modern methods the year of the birth of Takpiny's son was 1940. The Second World War was in its second year of progress. The village of Parial was in an atmosphere of merriment while Poland was traumatised by defeat.

The mother of Marial Takpiny, Alede Manyang Agok, with two daughters Akot and Ayen Takpiny, glorified and welcomed the healthy baby boy, me, into the family. The relatives in the surrounding village observed the event.

The cycle of life as described above went on normally in Parial village. A situation developed two years after weaning me. I became sick. I faced the turbulence without modern weapons, the drugs. From zero years to five years old is a dangerous range according to UN studies. The studies indicated many children south of the Sahara died below or at the age of five years. I was within the zone of death. The few lucky ones escaped. I was one of them.

The moment I felt unwell the best magicians of the area were summoned into action. A chance came to extract something from the paramount chief. The magicians went about doing their business. They started killing chickens, goats and bulls as offerings to whatever wanted to deprive me of life. My father was determined I would survive, the only son at that time, before my stepbrothers were born.

My sickness became the story of the year. The magicians tried herbs they knew that could cure. They presented themselves as lifesavers through their endeavours to make me continue to live. I became known to many people without them ever seeing me.

I came out of the death pattern of children south of the Sahara. The sequence of life in Parial went on as usual and people moved to the camps during the dry season and back to their villages at the beginning of the rainy season. A terrible misfortune that changed my life then happened. It devastated the Apar family, the Ajak section and the whole sub-district of Yirol. The turbulence was like a tsunami.

In about December or January, the traumatising event struck. We were in the Alualtok cattle camp in the toch. At three o'clock in the afternoon two uncles came from the village and were seated under a shed. My mother, Alede Manyang, Ametrun Dheng, my stepmother, another few people and myself went to greet the uncles. They broke the dreadful, alarming, tragic news that my father had died. That was as if they had thrown a stone into a flock of birds resting on the ground that took off with tremendous sound. The whole camp erupted into yells, screams and commotion.

The two uncles and other elders did all they could to control the members of the family from harming themselves, especially the two wives who wanted to finish themselves to the stage of inflicting physical harm. The two uncles, the wives and other people took off for the village. One of the uncles came back and got hold of me and followed the rest.

The group came late in the evening for the rituals to start. In the morning the rituals began. I was given a spear to spear a bull that was tied to a pole. It's a custom for the first bull to be speared by the first son. My spear didn't scratch the bull but it was speared to death by the elders. I was very small.

My first experience of death was that of my beloved father. I was lost and didn't know what to do. The whole area was as shocked as the American population were at the assassination of President J.F. Kennedy.

As time went by the family of Apar came out of shock. The chieftainship was a family affair, and Akuocpiir Malual Apar, the brother of Takpiny, was to be the chief of Ajak. He held the post for a short period and then died as suddenly as his brother during the rainy season. The death of dear uncle Akuocpiir happened when the majority of the people were in the villages. The news conveyed to us in the cattle camp. The reaction was the same as that of Takpiny. The family was overwhelmed and dismayed and the area traumatised. The people of the whole sub-district wondered and the same question was on their lips:

"What is happening to sons of Malual Apar?" Many unconvincing answers came up, such deaths easily determined in the first world or else people speculated and that's it.

Some weeks passed and somebody needed to be named as chief. The district authority would consult immediate relatives who would be predecessors of the deceased. The family of Apar decided on Dhieu Malual Apar, brother of Akuocpiir and Takpiny, to be the chief of the Ajak section. Let it be noted that the only three brothers of Malual Apar were from one mother, Deer Paceeu Yieng.

Uncle Dhieu Malual Apar accepted the decision of the family. The people became apprehensive that Dhieu Malual might meet the same fate as his brothers, who died respectively and within a short time of each other. The family of Apar brushed it aside. He held the job with determination.

He reformed the family of Apar by taking me to school. It was a magnificent decision. By then education didn't have roots in the South. Education in the South was left to missionaries and the Christian Church Missionary Society (CMS) opened schools in Lakes District as the South divided into church spheres: Catholic, Presbyterian and Anglican (Protestant). It is to be pointed out that pupils who dropped out from school didn't do well in a community. They became troublemakers and drunkards. As the English poet and satirist Alexander Pope said more than 200 hundred years ago, "A little knowledge is a dangerous thing." That behaviour vibrated in different communities in the South. The communities were discouraged and ignored the education being imparted by the church. School was seen as a place that corrupted children.

Apart from that, the British authorities didn't have jobs for students who might graduate from schools. There were no other local jobs. Positions of tribal court clerks were limited and no yearly intake existed.

Under such conditions there were no facilities. But the authorities became aware of such a precarious educational situation. It was planned to open an exemplary primary school for children of chiefs and noblemen. The plan wanted every child to bring a milking cow so that a child has some kind of a link with the cattle on which life was based.

Tonj Primary School was established in 1943 to open its doors to sons of chiefs, clan leaders and noblemen in 1944. A call went out to chiefs from the district commissioner to recruit boys to Tonj Primary School. There was a threat attached to that call, that any chief not fulfilling it would be punished. The authority warned the chiefs that a boy must be of good conduct.

The chiefs from Yirol responded. Those chiefs who didn't were asked to explain. My uncle Dhieu Malual told the assistant district commissioner that he had no son and his two brothers who held chieftainship before him didn't have sons to go to the school. He was told a boy of seven to ten years old would meet requirements.

The turbulence came. Somebody was sent to the cattle camp to bring me home to the village to be prepared by performing rituals. I was to be sent to another land, Tonj Primary School in the Tonj district, from the village and cattle camp life to school life. The village and the cattle camp life was the best I could think of and so I felt I was being deprived of a good life.

I travelled with my uncle Dhieu Malual, to Tonj, a distance of about 150 miles from home. The last words of my uncle when he said goodbye to me after he handed me to a big white man at the school compound were, "Son of my brother Takpiny, don't bring down the family of Apar. Chieftainship and cattle are nothing if you do well in school". There I was alone. I fought very hard to keep back the tears about to flow down my face. Later on I met boys from Yirol, Isaiah Kulang Mabor, John Rong, Alfred Acieng and George Garang Keny. That comforted me, after all I was not alone.

The words of my uncle became a challenge to me. They became an encouragement during those tender years of my growth. I reasoned that I would excel if I was to remain as a villager and cattle keeper. Now what would prevent me from excelling in the school?

At this juncture, it's necessary to mention three events that happened and influenced my life directly. I entered school in April 1947, Tonj Primary School, which was still being built, and so I was taught for six months under a big mahogany tree.

On 21 June 1947, the much talked about Juba Conference was held under the chairmanship of Civil Secretary Sir James W. Robertson, Esq. It was a window dressing and a sell-out of Southern Sudan. Mohammed Saleh Shingeiti, the advocate, together with Chairman Sir James Robertson, Esq, manoeuvred the unity of the South and the North.

In the same year the first secondary school moved from Atar in Upper Nile Province to Rumbek, chosen as it is ideally located at the centre of what is South Sudan today. The historic institution brought together students from different places of Southern Sudan. Unity of Southerners was forged in Rumbek Secondary School.

Chapter Three

Numeracy and literacy in exemplary school

Tonj Primary School wasn't an ordinary school. It existed to prove wrong the concept held by the Dinka people that school made a child ill-mannered and reckless, a drunkard and undisciplined. Trained teachers are appointed to impart appropriate learning. There is a military kind of discipline, such as if a bell rang to go to class or attend a parade, pupils ran as if chased by a wild beast. Being late to attend an occasion for no good reason meant a proper beating or other kind of punishments.

Prizes were awarded for achievements either academically or in body and clothes cleanliness. The school compound was kept clean, from classrooms to dormitories. Four sleeping rooms formed a block or a village. These villages competed and the object of the competition was an emblem of Bahr el Ghazal carved from wood. The pupils of the winning village marched through the other blocks singing songs of success, an exciting encounter for them and equally shameful for the other villages.

Once a month there would be a Sunday walk through the small town of Tonj. The pupils washed and ironed their uniforms to military standard as if the governor of the province was coming to inspect the guard of honour. Teachers, especially those on duty, would accompany pupils to the town.

The march was a military one with students marching in two parallel lines led by a band and students singing. The townspeople lined both sides of the road and shouted as the march moved on. All ages of people attended the entertaining occasion free of charge.

At the end of the year, villages which had won in activities and cleanliness awarded prizes to individual pupils and prefects. A prefect would get a heifer as an award to maintain the cultural link with cattle. Furthermore, academic achievers would go to a shop to choose cloth for a shirt and a pair of shorts. The awards motivated the pupils and for me they were coupled with the words of my uncle as quoted above. I collected some prizes and jumped classes. For example, I took a kangaroo leap from class one to class three in the primary school and from class two to class four in the intermediate school, and I then sat entrance examinations to the first senior secondary school in Southern Sudan, the historic RSSS.

The exemplary Tonj Primary School performed what it intended to impart, that is, numeracy and literacy to sons of chiefs and noblemen. It creates a gentleman's agreement between the chiefs and district authorities. The school was frequented by the district authorities who would meet with the headmaster so that he could inform them of the progress. It is their concern, the failure of the school to have serious implications to educational policy planned last time in the Sudan, the plan to leave a firm ladder of education established from primary to secondary.

The school aimed to graduate well rounded students and appropriate character behaviour would be instilled in its pupils.

From time to time the pupils remained from necessity in the community of discipline, honesty, manual work and respect to elders, each other and public materials. Abusive language was punishable. It was a small military model.

As the circumstances evolved, I was the first to be educated in the family of Apar, the first to go to school from the Ajak section. I was the first admitted to a government primary school, then the government intermediate school and then the historic secondary school. I was the pioneer in education institutions. My positive progress in educational institutions inspired other parents to take their children to school. Tonj Primary School had six year levels. The pupils then sit examinations to enter intermediate school. There is no government intermediate school in Bahr el Ghazal Province. Arrangements were made to avoid pupils returning to the villages or towns as this would reinforce the previous concept of the chiefs that school spoils pupils.

A ruling was made to change primary education from six years to four, thus becoming an elementary school. The sixth and fifth class were to sit the same examinations. The students of fifth class were alarmed about the combined examinations with the sixth form. Nothing could be done but to calm them down to sit the examination. The examination was in English, arithmetic and Dinka language. The achievers were to go to an intermediate school but not a mission intermediate school. We sat the examinations in 1949.

The students who passed the examinations were admitted to a class that was attached to Rumbek Secondary the previous year. Hence, there were two classes of intermediate level in RSSS and that was called junior secondary school.

I was in the experiment of the fifth year who sat examinations with the sixth year. I jumped from first year to third year and during my normal progress the change caught me in the fifth year. However, a good number of fifth year students made it and were accepted into Rumbek Junior Secondary School as first government intermediate school. The big boys of Rumbek Secondary School called boys from junior intermediate school "Blue Boys", the name they brought from Atar where they spent a year before transferring to Rumbek in 1947.

Of course, the junior secondary school had its own classrooms and the same teachers of senior secondary taught in the junior section. The standard was high. Another experiment was planned and implemented. The third year of junior section sat entrance examinations to RSS. That was the first government school in the province to compete with the mission intermediate schools of Loka, Okaru and Bussere. These mission intermediate schools were renowned academically. The third year students did well in the entrance examinations to Rumbek Secondary School and so the authority of Rumbek Secondary wanted to continue with the experiment.

The first twenty students plus older students from the second year junior section were promoted to fourth year to sit entrance examinations. The junior secondary school transferred in 1953 to Tonj, known as Tonj Intermediate School, the first government intermediate school in Southern Sudan. I was among those more than twenty students promoted to fourth year to continue the experiment, another kangaroo leap into another experiment. I became a student of examination experiments.

The pupils of Tonj Primary School aspired to gain admission to Tonj Intermediate School and it was the same for intermediate students wishing to obtain entrance to the school of distinction, RSSS. It needs to be mentioned that a sequence of an educational ladder was established and that is what the

British authority had hoped for in the South. Earlier on the British administration left education to the missionaries, but had second thoughts at the last moment not to leave it there. The British administration initiated public education before quitting the Sudan.

The experimental fourth year students in Tonj Intermediate School sat entrance examinations to the famous Rumbek Secondary School. A group of us passed the examinations and went back to Rumbek after a year in Tonj town in 1954. The competition to RSSS was stiff. Only thirty-five places, competed for by four intermediate schools, mainly Bussere, Loka, Okaru and Tonj. At the time facilities increased and acceptance rose to seventy students, two classes. The other students who passed entrance and couldn't be admitted to Rumbek Secondary were accepted to Juba Commercial Secondary School, JCSS, which replaced the former Juba Training Centre, JTC, a vocational institution that trained medical assistants, clerks, accountants and book-keepers.

The unity between North and South forged at the Juba Conference in 1947 exploded in an army mutiny in the Torit government garrison in August 1955. Rumbek Secondary School was hard hit, with two of its teachers killed in Lanya, 63 miles from Juba. One of the teachers killed was the assistant headmaster who was going with the fourth year students to tour Northern Sudan. Fate struck RSSS and it was not known how the mutiny would affect North and South in the future.

All educational institutions closed in the South and one academic year was lost as Rumbek Secondary, Juba Commercial and Maridi Teacher Training Institute transferred to Khartoum. The Northern Sudanese in Khartoum called students the sons of mutineers. The students were of different stock to the Northern Sudanese. The institutions had been moved to the South and back to the capital of Khartoum from time to time during civil war.

The Torit mutiny drew back my clock of advancement, putting me one year behind, and I graduated after five years. I finished RSSS in 1958 and was appointed as a teacher in an intermediate school in 1959.

Chapter Four

Career

Opportunity to get employment was extremely limited in the subsistence society of Southern Sudan. The government of the day was concerned with maintenance of law and order. Neglect of the region was a main factor. No jobs were available for graduates of secondary school except to be a teacher.

Names of students to attend an interview for scholarships abroad were announced over the government-owned Radio Omdurman. My name was there but I couldn't make it. Authorities responsible for scholarships would broadcast names and not care how far candidates had to travel to Khartoum. Places were limited and if some candidates didn't go that could be better for the Khartoum candidates.

However, my name appeared in another list of interviews stuck to the noticeboard of the department of education in Wau. I was nowhere to be located and never showed up for the interview. The department of education was desperate to get hold of me because of the great need for maths and science teachers. A chance to find me was slipping away. The academic year was about to terminate.

In the middle of November 1959 during a conversation, it came up that in April the education office wanted me.

Seven months after the interview a message came to me. Communication was to be blamed, but I decided to leave Yirol for Wau. One morning I went to the office knowing what was to be told to me. In the office I stood at attention before a desk, and behind it was a big brown man who looked to be tall.

Skinny as I was I still had not reached my maximum height of 194 cm by then. He looked up at me and said, "What do you want?" and with difficulty I managed to say, "My name is Martin Marial Takpiny". He replied, "What? Say it again". Before I could regain myself he said, "There is no stone left unturned". He got up, as tall as I expected and said to me, "Follow me". He led me to the office of the head clerk, who got up from his chair when we entered his office. He said, "This is Martin Marial, give him a letter of appointment addressed to the headmaster of Bussere North".

Later I learned his name to be Manoufi Effendi, the assistant education officer of Bahr el Ghazal Province. That's it, I was appointed as a teacher of government intermediate school and posted to Bussere North in November 1959.

Bussere, 12 miles south of Wau, was a mission school. The mission school was taken over by the government and became Bussere South Intermediate School. The two intermediate schools in the same area were now both government schools. It was the time lower school education expanded in the South.

As a young graduate, enthusiastic about my job, I carried a lot of teaching load, in maths, science and geography. There was a great need for teachers. I wanted to be exemplary in what I did, especially in discharging my duties.

I taught maths from second to fourth year, the fourth year students required to be properly prepared for the RSSS entrance examinations. Bussere North new school was to join stiff competition for entry to the only secondary school, Rumbek.

It was a challenge to both the teachers and students, especially when expected to perform miracles with some students who were mediocre for a variety of reasons.

In a classroom there are three types of standards: the cream of the class, the average group and the low achievers. An ideal teacher needs to be more concerned with the best few and the low achievers. The best few need to be kept at that level by encouraging them more and at the same time motivating the low achievers to cope with the classwork. A trained teacher doesn't neglect any student. Among them would be future leaders in different fields of knowledge. In one of my classes I had a young quiet student who distinguished himself in mathematics. He attracted my attention the very moment I started teaching in that class. In his exercise book of maths, three words alternated, "Excellent", "Splendid" and "Brilliant". These adjectives described his ability to handle mathematics.

That student was well rounded, good in all activities of the school. No wonder he became the charismatic leader who led Sudan's People's Liberation Movement and Sudan People's Liberation Movement Army and signed the magnificent Comprehensive Peace Agreement, or CPA, in 2005. He was John Garang de Mabior.

I spent three years teaching in Bussere North Intermediate School and was awarded a scholarship to the American University of Beirut in Lebanon in 1962. I graduated with a degree, a Bachelor of Arts, BA, in geography and Diploma of Education 1966. The university turned 100 years (established 1866). I continued with my studies as post graduate and obtained my Master of Arts, MA, in educational psychology in counselling and guidance in 1968. As a graduate I had access to reserve books in the upper sections of the big library. I made a discovery which kept me amused for some time in the library. When I laughed aloud, I made sure nobody was near me to avoid enquiries for why I was bursting into laughter.

It reminded me of an activity we did for almost 20 years in Tonj Primary School, the exemplary school. We were told to go under the huge mahogany tree in village two and we were then asked to move around, laugh in a wild manner, shout and create other forms of movements. The headmaster, Daniels Eric, Esq, present with another Englishman was taking pictures of us doing what we were told to do. All of us were naked.

My discovery was a small pamphlet-type book of pictures with captions of Tonj Primary School. Excited to see the title of the book I turned the pages. The book showed pictures of activities performed at that time. Two pictures electrified me: the photograph taken under the mahogany tree and the marching students. The naked students looked like leeches and I concentrated to try to discover myself in the pictures. I tried very hard but ended up laughing. My attempts were in vain although I paid attention to the area I thought I had been.

My focus was on the marching naked students led by student Arthur Agany Poole, carrying an emblem of Bahr el Ghazal Province. What interested me about the naked student Arthur Agany was that he was a product of an African woman and a European man. Arthur Agany couldn't be alienated from the culture of the nakedness of Dinka maternal uncles. The students started to wear clothes all the time as Sudan independence approached.

After six years in a university of reputation in the Middle East, the American University of Beirut, I went back to Sudan with degrees and a diploma of education. The rural boy from Parial Gok, the first educated person from Ajak and for that matter the first educated from the Apar family, had fulfilled the dream of his uncle Dhieu Malual Apar that I shouldn't let down the family.

Uncle Dhieu Malual the reformer and his sons, of whom one is a graduate of the University of Khartoum, John Buong Dhieu, and nephew, son of his brother Akuocpiir Malual Apar, medical doctor, Parmena Marial Akuocpiir, a graduate too. Cousins and nieces also attended school. The family of Apar becomes educated and Christian. Uncle Dhieu Malual deserved credit for his farsightedness and enlightenment.

Let me venture to say that the experiment of Tonj Primary School became a success, for three quarters of the graduates from exemplary school succeeded in education and in life. Many schools were modelled on the same way all over the province. The British administration policy of education was complete as RSSS successfully competed with senior secondary schools in the North. It took only a short time for RSSS to excel.

After graduation from the American University of Beirut I shifted to be a teacher of secondary school. Eventually I transferred to my old senior secondary, Rumbek, as a deputy headmaster. The school population expanded from a couple of hundred to more than a thousand students in 1972 after the Addis Ababa Agreement. A large number of student returnees were admitted to Rumbek. At that time there was no other senior secondary besides Rumbek. Without extension Rumbek Senior couldn't accommodate that number. School accommodation became a headache to the school authority under Franco Wel Garang, the headmaster.

With numerous students and administration problems, it dawned on me that the time had come to look for a better half. Miss Susan Ajak Simon Ngong Ayom accepted my proposal to spend the rest of our lives together. An engagement was declared according to the Dinka procedure of marriage. The marriage was negotiated at more than a hundred head of cattle, of which more than half was to be taken before the bride could go to the bridegroom.

Miss Susan Ajak was the daughter of Simon Ngong Ayom from Bor District in Upper Nile Province. The family of Ayom is a prestigious and large family of Alian, and bride wealth was high as the family is big. The two families of Ayom and Apar were perfectly matched.

Necessary arrangements were put in place and successfully implemented. Our wedding was conducted by Rev Enock Riak Magai in the Protestant church in Wau on 7 July 1973. I was galvanised and thrilled beyond belief. Happier than at my graduation from Rumbek Secondary School, happier than at my graduation with a Bachelor of Arts, happier than at my graduation with an MA. It was a special day for my wife and me when we made that vow: "to have and to hold from this day forward, for better for worse, in sickness and in health, to love and to cherish, till death us do part".

It needs to be mentioned here that those wonderful days were followed by another day in 1974 when our firstborn came joyfully into the world and we named him after the great man Takpiny. Our marriage was blessed by God at the hands of Rev Enock Riak Magai who celebrated the wedding and we were to bear seven living children and two deceased: Maker Marial Takpiny and Aluong Marial Takpiny. A third aborted, yet we have no regrets, for God gives and takes what is given. We divided our children with God.

My wife Susan Ajak Simon and I tried to orient our children to have a proper education which is a key to better life when it is coupled with better upbringing. That was our wish. And our children have not disappointed us.

Days after our wedding my wife and I went back to Rumbek. We, in our residence of deputy headmaster, began a new life. The residence was big for me before marriage and now real life was in the house.

However, I came back to Rumbek energised to tackle issues with vigour. There was more concentration on my duties because I felt well rounded. RSSS became a home to me. I studied at the junior secondary school attached to RSSS. As a student from 1954 to 1959, one year was lost as explained elsewhere in the book. Then I became an administrator and a teacher. Everything on the school compound was familiar to me, including the trees and flowering bushes. That wasn't all; I became a commissioner (1979-1981) of the Lakes Province, created after the former Bahr el Ghazal Province was split into two in 1976. RSSS fell under my jurisdiction with its many student problems. That added to my experience of RSSS.

As a normal cycle in educational institutions, I was transferred to Malakal Teachers Institute of Education. Many parts of the Upper Nile Province land are clay soil that cracks during the dry season and becomes sticky mud during the rainy season. Malakal town situated along the White Nile has clay soil. When encountering it for the first time, mud repulses a newcomer in Malakal town. Everywhere after rain is water and mud. Once a person becomes familiar with the mud and flooding they become barely aware of all that. Cost of living outside Juba, the capital of South Sudan has always been cheap, Malakal included. And that pins down people living in those areas. It is near the granary of Renk area, there is plenty of fish and cattle are kept within the vicinity to provide the town with milk. Thus, being cheap compensated for mud and flood water.

Malakal town didn't pin me down for more than a year and I went back to the Regional Ministry of Education in Juba. In the ministry, my job description dealt with planning and establishment of the map location of schools according to population dispersal all over the South. Lower school education expanded rapidly as demand dictated. The parents came to understand the importance of education because exemplary school alerted them and regional government manned exclusively by Southerners encouraged and motivated fathers and mothers to allow children to attend school to be like so and so in the government. The children sent to relatives working in towns created social and financial problems to the carers of these children in the town.

Many primary schools planned and estimated to meet the demands of the people in the rural areas. Schools were to be taken to children in the rural communities rather than children going to towns to schools. A large number of returnees from refuge in East Africa needed to be educated and pressured the ministry even more. Primary education is a function of intermediate and secondary. That plan meant more intermediate and secondary schools initiated to have a ladder of education. It must be emphasised that expansion couldn't proceed without teachers or manpower. Shortage of teachers became acute at all levels of education. At the same time the Regional Ministry of Education was very mindful of standards.

Two delegations led by regional ministry went to Egypt to create cooperative relationships between the young Regional Government of Southern Sudan and the developing country of Egypt. The author was a member of the two delegations which visited Egypt at different times. Education needs of the South came up both for teachers and further education. There were two protocols signed, whereby a number of Egyptians were appointed to teach in the South and 300 graduates of senior secondary school were to be admitted to Egyptian institutions every academic year. The admission to Egyptian institutions was more than ten times the number of Southerners in Sudanese institutions of education.

Each province of Bahr el Ghazal, Equatoria and Upper Nile apportioned 100 places to compete for the Egyptian institutions. Equatoria had a large number of student returnees and filled its places one hundred percent. Bahr el Ghazal sent seventy-five percent of its quota and Upper Nile abused its quota with only fifty percent admitted and that disappointed education authorities in Juba. However, the covenant that benefited the South was cancelled by the government of President Omar Hassan Ahmed el Bashir for reasons not farfetched.

The regional government passed a law to teach developed Southern languages in the first and second years of primary school. An organisation called the Summer Institute of Linguistics (SIL) invited to help the Regional Ministry of Education with its developed and undeveloped languages. It took a lot of time to convince security organs to allow the SIL to come to Sudan.

The planning department made headway with the security organs to allow the SIL to operate. The department organised accommodation at those areas of performance, Palotaka from the start, then Boma, Mbile and its headquarters at Maridi Institute of Education.

The planning department presented a lot of justification explanations to security. The SIL had a small plane (one engine) and communication sets (radios) at Boma, Mbile, Maridi and the Regional Ministry of Education. The timing was sensitive because Addis Ababa Agreement had just concluded and the SIL was seen as an intelligence agency and the author as the head of the planning department was subjected to all kinds of queries. The department had nothing to fear or hide. No doubt the SIL and the Regional Ministry of Education were kept under constant surveillance by security in Juba and Khartoum. The usual suspicion between South and North propelled frequent queries.

Above all, political discontent built up and when the first bullet was released in army garrison in Bor it served as an escape mechanism which exploded and echoed at various places in the South. The security found a pretext to commandeer the communication sets and the SIL personnel became the first refugees from the South in Kenya.

Let it be remembered that politics attracted officials like the author during that period. There have been issues coming up from time to time in the political arena where one would feel the need to contribute.

Chapter Five

Politics

Politics in the Southern Sudan came into being with the Juba Conference in 1947. The conference convened to sound out opinion of the South through chiefs brought to represent it. However, Sir James Robertson, Esq, the Civil Secretary and Judge Shingeiti with their hidden agenda coached southern representatives to believe that the South would be more comfortable as a part of the Middle East.

Southern politics developed by the appearance of two main parties in the 1960s: The Southern Front which stood for "self-determination" that was farfetched at that time and Sudan African National Union, Sanu, urging all Africans to form a union to become one big effective party and form a government. It needed tremendous work but was not impossible. Sanu stood for a federal system which would protect the rights of the marginalised Sudanese people.

The two objectives of the two parties became reality in the twenty-first century. The non-African Sudanese became apprehensive of the two parties and laboured very hard so that no party among the two would achieve its objective. The non-African Sudanese advanced three policies on Arabism, Islamism and head-knocking among Southern politicians. The ruling non-African presented themselves to the Arabs as Arabs and spent a huge amounts of dollars in order to be heard and accepted by the Arabs. For example, Sudan sent its forces along the Suez Canal zone during the 1967 Seven-Day War to fight Israel. The non-African Sudanese propagated extremely hard to let Sudan be acknowledged as an Islamic country (compare Turkey and Sudan). The non-African Sudanese skilfully put Southerners at odds with each other. The programme worked as could be seen in 2011 but is not a subject of this book.

As politics progressed, scepticism expressed by southern chiefs in 1947 grew and eventually exploded in military confrontation in August 1955 in an army garrison of Torit that led to guerrilla warfare. The Addis Ababa Agreement was reached and the South granted local autonomy. Regional government managed by the High Executive Council, HEC, was manned by members of the Southern Front and Sanu.

During frequent elections in the whole of Sudan, a person participated in the South as either a member of the Southern Front or Sanu. I was a sympathiser of the Southern Front and left teaching. I became a member of the Regional Assembly from 1978-1984 as a backbencher, later appointed as commissioner for the Lakes province, a status of state minister. I served two terms as the commissioner of Lakes Province, first under the President of the High Executive Council, Joseph Lagu Yanga and then a second term during Abel Alier Kwai's second term at the HEC.

The Sanu sympathisers understood that Lakes Province needed to be governed by a Sanu man or opposition to another party man. Aware of that attitude, I went with determination to do what was required of me. The president of HEC wanted people to be served regardless of political, colour, their linguistic or political affiliation.

My predecessor, a Sanu stalwart, laid down a network of Sanu political mines. I walked into a den of lions in Rumbek and Tonj. The two districts closed the Sanu area and the sympathisers planned to make the districts ungovernable to fail me, a naive and unsophisticated thinking of the time.

Two factors encouraged my government to be vigilant a few months before I could come, a tribal fight between the Apaak section and a section of Agar of Akot and Pacong. Security became a top priority in the province. No sooner did I come to Rumbek than I set up a special court with chiefs from Tonj and Gogrial and centre of the court in Akot. I opened the court's first session. The court was to determine causes of the fight, the ringleaders of the fight on both sides of Apaak and Agar and to find who had killed who. Those killed on both sides were to have compensation paid to relatives.

I attended half of the first session. Responsibility for persons killed was accepted by those who killed them. One name interested me, the name of Malueel. The question was posed by an Apaak man, who killed warrior Malueel? A well-built young man stood up as the killer of Malueel. A whisper went around among the Apaak. One Apaak man got up and said, "Yes, Malueel cannot be killed by a simple man except for a person of your physique". The Apaak group gave a sigh of approval for confession.

The evening the fight began, the Apaak were dispersed by the Agar and Apaak women yelled: "Malueel da Wee! Malueel da Wee!" The Agar took it to mean they had killed a brave famous person and the women mourned for him. The Agar waited anxiously throughout the night. The Apaak would avenge brave Malueel.

Surprised and amused, I kept it to myself because I knew the story of Malueel. Malueel, a Ciec man, (Dinka) was killed by the Apaak a long time ago at a toch between Ciec and Apaak and that toch was given the name of Malueel. Philosophically when "Malueel da Wee" is yelled, it is as if the toch does not exist any longer. It is a warning to regroup and return to fight.

However, Malueel was compensated with the rest who had been killed. The court proceeded normally and peace prevailed in the province.

The other factor taking my time was hunger in the province. The moment I was appointed commissioner I went to Renk, the granary of the South, to arrange purchase and transport of grain to the province. Rumbek and Tonj (in the years to come to be known as Warrap) amalgamated and became a vast province. Supplies flowed through the river port of Shambe and Wau railway terminus. The area was well serviced.

The opposition of the Sanu group in Rumbek and Tonj went beyond expectations. It is normal that a ruling party be reminded of its shortcomings and corrected should need be. The Sanu supporters were not thinking along those lines.

There was an action planned in Rumbek to be hatched in Tonj. As a new commissioner I had to visit all my constituencies to meet the population for them to see me in person. I went to Tonj town and a reception party was carried out. The dancing was in full swing when fishing spears, stones and sticks began to rain down onto the persons on the stage. The intention was to hurt, to kill and that was the motive. Sadly, for the planners and fortunately for us nobody was hit. The party was stopped by security personnel.

In the morning elders came to me to ask for amnesty for what happened the previous night. I told them to take it easy as I took it simply as being executed by thugs, misguided and common criminals.

That wasn't it, and next worshippers were attacked in the mosque. The president of HEC, Abel Alier Kwai, and I flew to Tonj. We met merchant groups from the North and assured them that it wouldn't be repeated. Khartoum took it seriously that Northerners were prosecuted in the South.

The wish of the planners of those incidents was to remove the commissioner and to bring in a Sanu man, which didn't happen. It seemed the bosses of Sanu didn't bless personality elimination because it might boomerang. Nevertheless, attempts of elimination practised in the Tonj district almost succeeded but the consequences wouldn't have been pleasant.

A general reshuffle returned me to the backbench of the Regional Assembly in Juba, but soon political intrigues initiated in the North were quickly reflected in the South. The Regional Government which first came into being in 1972 was divided into three governments of the previous provinces of Bahr el Ghazal, Equatoria and Upper Nile. The people of Equatoria believed that "Kokora" (said to be a Bari word for division). The word has since acquired political connotations as used and understood by both opponents and supporters of two camps: the grouping that was advocating that South should remain as a one entity and be collectively accountable to the central government in Khartoum whose bullying they feared. On the other hand, proponents of Kokora, most of them from Equatoria, wanted each of the former provinces of Bahr el Ghazal, Equatoria and Upper Nile to be responsibly individually to Khartoum. They argued that such an arrangement would curb what they perceived as monopoly of power by larger communities, particularly the Dinka.

It's disseminated that the South was given what it had been calling for, federalism. The stage of federalism had been overtaken by the events of the time. In essence, the local autonomy was federalism, but the ruling elites in the North refused to call it by its real name.

Smart thinkers in Khartoum worked very hard to abrogate the Addis Ababa Accord. No sooner that was done than the Bor army garrison mutinied and that news reached me in Juba's maximum security prison. I was arrested in Rumbek town on my way to Juba, just a day after President Jaafar Mohammed Nimeiri had an encounter with students of RSSS. The president visited Rumbek thinking that he was still the darling of the South. He never gave a thought that because he had abrogated the Addis Ababa Accord valued very much by the South the students shouted him down and abusive slogans were exhibited to him and his entourage. It was unthinkable and somebody must pay for those students' hostilities.

The president was hurt and left Rumbek town. The population of Rumbek, the provincial capital felt guilty, especially the commissioner, Peter Muoranyar Biet, of Lakes Province. The president's visit lasted some bitter hours in Rumbek and he was reported as having left without eating.

Late in the afternoon, the same day the president departed, I came from Wau en route to Juba via Yirol and spent the night in Rumbek town. In the morning at about seven I went on my way but before I could leave the town a young police officer rushed after my car and stopped me. He politely asked me to follow him to the police station. Being a law abiding citizen, I went to the station without comments or questions.

I was escorted to prison, a place where I visited prisoners occasionally and gave them gifts. I was a prisoner in a place I was an authority. The order of the day was to shame, scare and intimidate. The population in Rumbek town was shocked, bewildered and puzzled.

President Nimeiri came to Rumbek while I was in Wau, 140 miles from Rumbek. The communications were not so well developed as to incite students of Rumbek Senior Secondary

School to demonstrate against him. It was coincidence that the president arrived the previous day and I transited the town the following day.

What is obvious to me and the citizens of Rumbek town was that the commissioner, Peter Muoranyar Biet, wanted a scapegoat to disclose to the president and security in Khartoum that the organiser, the culprit was locked behind bars in Rumbek maximum security prison. The commissioner had to give a plausible tale to prolong his internship as a commissioner. A number of teachers and leading personalities were locked up to make the window dressing seem real.

Eventually four of us were transferred under heavy escort to Juba prison. No charges of any offence were laid and no records of misdeeds taken. I was to be released after six months in prison without charges, thought to have sufficiently intimidated me according to security organs.

One day I was summoned to the office of head of security in Juba. That was the worst I had experienced since the arrest. I was told in no uncertain terms that whenever I decided to leave Juba I had to inform the security office of all details of my journey and report my arrival at the other end. A storm started within me, which I suppressed, and I made sure I did not make a face to the officer or I would be exiled behind prison bars for a longer period. Treatment of blacks during apartheid flashed into my mind. The phrase that "colonialism has no colour" dominated my thoughts. I was convinced beyond doubt that the security men could do anything to me since details of my movements were to be lodged with them. Is there anything worse than that in a country claiming to be democratic? As mentioned above, guerrilla warfare activities were in progress in eastern Upper Nile. However, I bore the situation for more than a decade until the time was right to respond.

Chapter Six

Academic life

I lost interest in politics, but national and regional parliaments interrupted me from time to time. Political power struggle in the North affected affairs in the South. There was no political stability and continuity and the situation became worse in the South with resources controlled by the North.

A university came into existence in the middle of Juba town. It was installed on the compound of an intermediate school. More buildings were constructed to accommodate university facilities such as large lecture halls, laboratories, a big library and staff houses. It was co-sponsored by an infant regional government and the European Community, the predecessor of the European Union, which shouldered large portions of the expenses.

It needed lecturers in all fields, especially Sudanese. Foreign lecturers were recruited and paid by the European Union. My academic credentials entitled me to a lectureship. With an MA in educational psychology counselling and guidance and a diploma in education, I could teach general psychology, educational subjects and counselling guidance, my main subjects. Counselling guidance helps students match academic performance with their intended desired career. It is common for students to aspire to jobs they don't have the potential for. Hence the necessity of a counsellor to help students with such issues. Mainly first year students tend to have such problems.

I joined the University of Juba in 1985 after I graduated from the Rumbek and Juba prisons. I thought the security would leave me alone and that was a misconception. The government of the day was the National Congress Party, NCP, which, according to members of the party, would rule Sudan for as long as possible, if not for ever. The party wanted to make sure that every ministry was led by their party man and the personnel of the ministry would be party persons by all means. A student charity fund (sanduk da'm el thulab) was set up in every educational institution to provide food for students instead of using contractors and to give security men an opportunity to monitor the activities of staff, students and workers of every institution in the Sudan. Arop Madut Arop expressed what the National Islamic Front, NIF, did more forcefully:

> NIF... infiltrated the institutions of the state including military, trade unions, teachers, workers, farmers, banking and other financial institutions... NIF infiltrated the students' unions at different levels of education with a neo-fundamentalist missionary zeal.
> (Arop, Madut Arop, *Sudan's Painful Road to Peace*, page 187, 2006.)

Professor Moses Macar Kacuol was the vice chancellor of the University of Juba, when I became a member of the university academic staff. He was a hardworking man, dedicated to his obligations and objectives. He had little taste for politics though was dragged into it by the NIF, desperate to engage Southerners of esteem into the government.

Prof Kacuol became the first high ranking victim of arrest in the university. No charges of arrest were stated except for public interest, an empty phrase for no specific allegations used by security organs. Three reasons were speculated for his detention, the first to warn the population of the university that nobody was above the law. Secondly, he would be softened by NIF watchdogs. Thirdly, he might have been overheard saying disagreeable statements. Thus he was taken to the notorious ghost house where unfortunate men lost their lives.

There was an outcry from non-NIF staff, students, workers and respectable Southern politicians added to that outcry from the University of Juba. After all, no crime had been committed, just security laws cited in order to arrest and scare citizens.

Before the University of Juba could finish welcoming back Professor Moses Macar Kacuol from detention, another bomb was thrown into the university compound. It was my time to be terrified for a second time as the security men felt that the six months I spent in prison in the South in 1983 didn't frighten me. The security thought I recollected myself and should be shaken up more and therefore arrested.

I was taken to that dreaded ghost house at night while the rest of the detainees slept. In the morning I met five Southerners. It was forbidden to speak to each other except to nod. Before breakfast we prepared vegetables for the day's meals. That was the time we could talk a little bit. At times we'd sit in a circle with an opened Bible as though discussing or reading the Bible. That was the only times to exchange views.

During my first arrest in Rumbek, I finished reading the entire Bible. It is a good book of literature of life to read at times of sadness and pleasure. During my reading of it I rediscovered Joseph was sold for thirty pieces of silver by his brothers. I concluded that the commissioner arrested me to buy favour from President Nimeiri.

Nobody taught my classes in my absence and the students were at the point of physical confrontation among themselves, those pro and against my detention. It could have turned ugly and the security backed down. As usual, no charges had been levelled against me and I spent about a week there and was then released. The security men scored an objective of intimidation. I was told to report to the security office for a period of time. I would sit outside the security office to be told to go home later. It eventually stopped but added to my bitterness.

It was a process of instilling fear, a psychological conditioning, a scheme or method to break a person mentally. The detentions that happened in the University of Juba occurred when the university moved from Juba to Khartoum. The NIF took over the government in 1989 with the main goal to defeat the SPLM/A. A brutal clash occurred in and around Juba town while the University of Juba had already evacuated to Khartoum.

As the turbulence subsided in the University of Juba, another was gathering strength somewhere. Military and political heat became hotter and the government sought an escape mechanism. The University of Bahr el Ghazal was announced to be established and Professor Moses Macar Kacuol was to implement it. It opened in Khartoum with three colleges of health science (medicine and veterinary), economics and education. The government put pressure on the vice chancellor to take the university to Wau town. It served the government as a propaganda scheme that the SPLM/A was being defeated. It sounded magnificent to the government to talk of SPLM/A "defeat" and it was a nightmare physically.

The dedicated Professor Vice Chancellor Moses Macar Kacuol took the challenge wholeheartedly and went to Wau to make ready the intermediate schools at the centre of Wau town to shelter the college of education. He found accommodation but needed somebody to administer the college in Wau.

Wau town was surrounded by very aggressive battalions of SPLA which made sure that the government army couldn't move out of it at will. Any military convoy travelling to an outlying garrison needed to be well equipped with military hardware, officers, soldiers and brave determined officers to take a convoy to that particular town. Even the vehicle to be in front caused lot of talking into and persuasion of drivers. The chances of a convoy getting safely to its destination was always in the balance and either arrived with heavy losses of men and materials or dispersed.

It is not an exaggeration to say that Wau town was an open prison without walls for those residents. The situation worsened from year to year. That's the town the college of education tried to function within. Some of the nights seemed like active fronts during the Second World War when all guns would shoot, either at the illusion of an enemy or out of sheer fear.

The college needed a resolved person to lead teachers and students to the frontline garrison of education. The vice chancellor of the University of Bahr el Ghazal asked for my transfer there. Promoted to associate professor I took up my duties as the dean of the college of education in Khartoum. The teachers and students were expected in Wau town at any time.

No hotels in El Obeid could accommodate more than fifty students and teachers en route to Wau. It would be expensive to spend a night in El Obeid town. One late afternoon we crammed into a bus and travelled throughout the night to arrive early in the morning at El Obeid airport to board a plane to Wau under the watchful eyes of security men.

The college of education functioned in Wau as planned. I managed to spend four painful years there. It was a challenge to me. The teachers resolved to teach under hard conditions of insecurity and the students were determined to learn in that alarming atmosphere. The teachers taught and the students learned at the expense of their existence. It was a tragedy that the vice chancellor urged the opening of a college of education at that time in Wau, the frontline town. However, it was a kind of blackmail to the vice chancellor, the dean of the college, teachers and students alike because there was a latent threat.

The teachers and students were exposed to all kinds of hazards such as when a plane crashed, with fifteen students from the college of education among the dead. The plane attempted to land in a dust storm and crashed over Khartoum. It was tragic and left the population of the college of education devastated and demoralised. It was extremely hard to cope with it. I was personally hurt and felt guilty. They were my sons, metaphorically speaking.

More risks were to come and nothing except luck and fortune helped save Wau town from a well-coordinated attack and capture in 1997. It was a challenge to do the impossible under the circumstances. Preparations were completed to graduate fourth year students in Wau. The population in the town was waiting in anticipation of the graduation. The necessary arrangements were made on the compound and the populace waited excitedly for the day to come.

At the last moment I was instructed to transport the students to Khartoum to graduate there. Wau town became terribly insecure for guests and delegates from Khartoum. Before

I could start the transportation of students, the unexpected happened.

The head of the charity fund, sanduk da'm el thulab was a thorn in my side. In the absence of the vice chancellor he felt he could do anything, especially to make use of the vice chancellor's car. He looked at me with contempt and I strongly suspected he made a file for me with the security due to my uncooperative attitude.

My colleague, Ali Tamim Fartak, the governor of Bahr el Ghazal, once intimidated me in his office in the presence of a security officer. Not only that, in a public rally he called upon security organs to screen the University of Bahr el Ghazal, pointing to the compound. I wanted to go to him and ask what the university had done that he had to announce in the rally to let security pay attention to it. I was persuaded to get a copy of his recorded speech. Unfortunately, that part was erased from the tape.

The utterances of the governor of the province, the authority of the territory, would drive the security men to deal with me. The security would strike at any time in a manner that suited them. I had no protection and no alternative but to wait for my day of execution.

Wau people became apprehensive of my life. The statement of the governor Ali Tamim Fartak was a death sentence. The security needed just to interpret it. Nevertheless, Governor Ali Tamim and I were one-time members of the Southern Front. He was from Raga constituency, appointed commissioner of Bahr el Ghazal Province, and I was commissioner of Lakes Province. That was the second period of Abel Alier Kwai's presidency of the HEC. I found him a different man, a diehard of the NCP. Maybe Ali Tamim carried out the policy of the NIF to subdue every person with different views.

The attention shifted from me very fast. East of Bahr el Ghazal Province was a de facto SPLM/A territory. The unexpected event came into existence and traumatised citizens in Wau. The Wau airport closed to prevent the people from leaving, and that frightened and demoralised soldiers in the military garrison in Wau. I negotiated with the military commander to allow students to be rushed away from the shaken area. The presence of idle and frightened students combined with the general fear that gripped the town.

The commander of Bahr el Ghazal Province allowed students and staff to be airlifted from Wau. I would be the last to leave. The capture of Rumbek and Tonj military garrisons by the SPLA happened like lightning, a blitzkrieg that shocked and shook the government NIF in Khartoum. The blitzkrieg spread like a wild Australian bushfire that jumped across highways. Within a short while Gogrial military garrison was seized by SPLA fighters and slipped into its strong jaws.

Wau town was in a panic and nobody contemplated the hostile SPLA forces would be repulsed with ease. A word came to citizens of Wau to remain in town at their own expense. The message was clear and full of danger for each individual to digest. It would be difficult to attack army soldiers scattered all over the town to secure it. That was an army tactic of human shields. An SPLA bullet wouldn't discriminate a soldier from an innocent civilian.

At long last the time came to make a decision that could change my life for better or worse. I reflected on my poor relations with the governor Ali Tamim Fartak and the head of school's sanduk da'm el thulab. That was sufficient to make me a victim of crossfire between the army and the SPLM/A, a threat of danger as clear as daylight. The situation became apparent not to take chances or gamble with my life.

The governor suspected me to be a sympathiser of the SPLM/A, and I assumed him to have communicated his thoughts to his watchdogs. The security mistrust of the population ensured the citizens assumed to be followers of the SPLM in town were rounded up and arrested. A state of emergency prevailed whereby one could be apprehended and made to stay in custody for a long time. The arrested persons were tortured to death in many cases. Many of us were legitimate targets of the security men.

As events unfolded rapidly with the success of the SPLA forces in taking Rumbek and Tonj, I received a strong warning from my relatives, who were in contact with the security circle, that it would only be a matter of days before I would be taken into custody. The warning was an alarm to my family and they asked me to act before it was too late.

The warning of my impending arrest was crystal clear and the consequences known. It wouldn't be like the detention of Rumbek town in 1983 or that of Khartoum in 1993. The pending apprehension would have serious results for me. I made a decision with my wife and our two elder daughters to leave for an SPLM/A held area. After weighing other options, we could not wait for an SPLA attack and we didn't know how it would end. There was no time to waste to put into action our plan of escape from this open prison without walls. We made sure that our movements or intentions were not known to anybody.

Let me take you back a little bit. It was like in 1995 when we kept secret the journey of my son Takpiny Marial Takpiny to Syria in the Middle East. The civil war became intensive and male persons more than ten years old were recruited into the army to fight the SPLA. My son could be recruited at any time to fight his relatives and friends in the SPLA. My wife and

I made a difficult decision to send him to Syria, not knowing how he would fare there. We preferred it that way rather than him to be in the army where his chances of survival were rather remote.

In the Middle East he made his way to Canada with the help of his maternal uncle, Mabuto Simon Ngong. Very little contact was maintained with him, but we knew that he was alive somewhere in Canada.

It took 13 years to establish a link with him. In 2008 a drama happened. One morning at about 11.00 am Australian Eastern Time, somebody knocked at our door and I opened it. I saw a tall person of my physique and I shouted and rushed to him. We shouted at each other with joy. The rest of the family joined us and there was commotion in the residence. That was our family reunion with our son, Takpiny. The reception was like that of the prodigal son in the Bible except Takpiny was sent away for security reasons. The family reunited in Sydney, NSW, Australia. When we left Wau town we divided in two with my wife going with our children and I going alone. Each could face any situation, our great hope only for reunion. We united again after one day's separation. The reunion of the family occurred with jubilation in an SPLM/A held area.

The crossing points along the river to the SPLM/A held area were closely watched throughout. Large numbers of people from the town were leaving for rural areas. It was imminent that the SPLA would attack the town at an opportune time. The town was gripped by panic and fear. Furthermore, the security in the town was extremely precarious and critical. The armed forces were nervous and considered everybody in the town to be SPLA soldiers.

Our zero hour to escape came on Tuesday 27 May 1997 when we left Wau town. It was very painful to me. We walked into an uncertain future than face unknown circumstances in Wau, where some men planned to get rid of me from this earth.

A rendezvous was agreed upon and my family was to spend the night in a disused Wau canning factory in Agok. My daughters walked to the rendezvous in twos and mother went alone to reach Agok, the rendezvous focal point. They left in the late afternoon for the place to spend the night in order to cross the river very early in the morning, before security men came to screen who was leaving town. I remained in our residence to sneak out later on in the evening at about 8:00pm local time. I crossed to the SPLM/A area under cover of darkness. That night the moonlight was so bright that one could see minute objects around. It's as if nature cooperated with the security men to make the sky clear of clouds to ensure that no escapees would leave the town that night, but I was determined to get free from Wau despite the risks.

I became what's officially called an internally displaced person, IDP. Forced out of my natural habitat in Wau, I ended up in Achana, a village outside of Wau which was an IDP centre. I left Wau voluntarily to be free from humiliation, torture and eventually to be released from prison, dying from what had been done to me. The death would then be described as normal. Many people released from arrest have gone through that death.

The commanding officer of SPLA forces in Achana, Commander Ajongo Mawut, my former student in an intermediate school, interviewed me as a matter of formal procedure since I came from a town under control of the government. After my chat with Commander Ajongo Mawut, he offered me a goat for my consumption with my family at the civil side of Achana. That was humility from Commander Ajongo Mawut who still remembered the student-teacher good old days.

He radioed my arrival into the SPLM/A arena, to Commander-in-Chief the late Dr John Garang de Mabior, my former student in Bussere Intermediate School. The commander-in-chief of SPLA and chairman of SPLM in turn informed all units that I had joined the movement. I was a high ranking official of the government of Sudan.

There was a big force in Achana. The Sudan government army prepared to attack. Trenches were dug and aerial bombardment was anticipated. It was an unsafe place to stay for long and I asked for what was called "departure orders", a protection from other SPLA soldiers I might meet. A junior officer assigned two guards to accompany me since my daughters could be targets of some irresponsible soldiers and men. One could not rule out that during war, the law of jungle prevailed. Nobody wanted to take any risks.

Our large group consisting mainly of women and children left on foot for Tonj. No other means of communication or transport were available except to walk. Roads were heavily mined and infrastructure destroyed. It was not an easy exercise to walk a distance of 100 kilometres through forest following a footpath. We drank from waterholes containing disease bearing water.

We depended on ourselves and each of my daughters carried a few clothes, a little food and a few cooking utensils. I carried my water thermos. That was all we had in the world for we left everything in the town. Our sole goal was to survive.

It took nine days of hard walking to reach Tonj. My feet were blistered and painful to walk on. I had no choice but to persevere and to have low spirits would discourage my wife and children. Since we set off we were ready for any eventualities. It's better to have blistered feet than to be tortured and killed in cold blood. My family inspired me to have courage.

They showed no sign of despair either spiritually or physically, especially my youngest, Atong Marial who was four years old at that time. It has to be mentioned that we were not aware that our destiny was going to be tens and tens of thousands of kilometres away, and where was it?

After two days my cousin Michael Manoah, an SPLA officer, arranged my transport with my family to Rumbek. The government garrison was smashed on 1 May 1997. The town was ruined and the population dispersed into surrounding villages as the SPLA soldiers became the inhabitants. I couldn't describe the destruction of the town. It had become a forest. I spent two gloomy days under a group of mango trees in front of my previous office (the provincial commissioner's office) near a big well-constructed bunker of the NIF forces.

The town was not safe and there was nowhere to reside so we decided to proceed to a village where my relatives welcomed me. My cousin, Daniel Ayual Makoi, accommodated me in the village of Madet in the Rorkec area of Yirol county. The area was far from the government garrison in Yirol. My relatives lived from near Yirol to the Rorkec section northwest of Yirol town.

After some time, I moved to a church accommodation in Mapuordit village. Arrangements were made by other cousins, Daniel Makur Dol, and Gabriel Gak Athong, an evangelist. I had peace of mind in the village compared to mental pressure in Wau, with no worries from security, which used to monitor all that I did.

Chapter Seven

A refugee in East Africa

However, the blisters on my soles of my feet developed into wounds and couldn't be dressed because of lack of medications in the village. The diabetic drugs were finished and there was nowhere to purchase them. My wife urged me to leave for Kenya for treatment and if possible to look for a job. In short there were no services in the village: no education, no health care, little food, no clean drinking water and no sanitation. The citizens looked to the World Food Programme, WFP to provide food. War had ravaged villages and towns and famine prevailed.

There was severe drought and no cultivation of food crops. I learned later on in Nairobi of the unique weather condition called El Nino that occurred at the Horn and Central Africa. Heavy clouds appeared as if heavy rain would come but were driven off. It prevailed from 1997 to 1998 and hunger dominated the region.

I listened to my wife and travelled to Kenya, leaving the family in Mapuordit. My wife became strong and determined to keep our children alive by going to any centre in the vicinity where there was food brought in by the WFP. Necessity drove her to cover long distances on foot to fetch food and carry it back on her head to our children. Such an experience was completely new to her but she never gave up. Her life was exposed to wild animals, landmines and robbers who wandered around the centres of food distribution. One time a landmine exploded under a lorry she was on yet she was unhurt. The vow we made to each other during our marriage ceremony to be together in every good or bad situation was holding firm.

With courage and commitment, she established her compound, cultivated food crops and became stable in Mapuordit village. In Kenya I became a refugee, not an IDP. I had crossed an international border to become a refugee.

David Deng Athorbei gave me shelter in his residence in Nairobi. Lack of medications in the village made my diabetes aggressive to me. I became very weak, lost a great deal of weight and sick. David Deng Athorbei helped direct me to good doctors. The diabetes subsided and I put on weight, thanks to David Deng.

It was difficult to be employed being a refugee, despite my academic qualifications. A refugee is reduced to the lowest level of his or her previous activities and can only fulfil a bare minimum of needs.

Once I left Wau in May 1997 I moved southwards until I reached Mapuordit village, where we settled temporarily. I continued my journey south alone until I reached Kenya. I left no stone unturned to find a job in a foreign country from the available simple manual work able to be given to refugees. Fortunately, in 1998 I worked with the New Sudan Council of Churches (NSCC) behind SPLM/A lines. It was established to accommodate refugees in East Africa and served IDPs in SPLM/A held areas in the South. NSCC, the counterpart of Sudan Council of Churches, SCC, served under the Sudan government. In essence NSCC was a church organisation run by Southerners in Nairobi. It provided humanitarian assistance to the war affected people of Southern Sudan. The NSCC was headed by an ordained priest and at the time of my appointment it was the executive secretary Rev Dr Harun Run Lual, a native of Melut County in northern Upper Nile.

The NSCC, like a conventional government ministry, had departments of finance, education, information, legal affairs and aid. Each department was headed by an officer. All the departments were headed by Southern Sudanese except education, which was under a Kenyan. The whole organisation depended solely on donations from world Christian denominations mainly from the Western world. The officers wrote projects to attract funding from non-government organisations, NGOs and many of them contributed generously. Unicef, a leading contributor to educational projects of schools, facilitated and functioned better in areas of the South controlled by SPLM/A than those schools under the Government of Sudan in the South.

The education department of the NSCC had several responsibilities:

1. Education survey to cover assessment of education needs and capacities of the region.
   a) To design and develop a plan for education programs to be conducted by the churches in the region;
   b) To monitor the educational needs and progress;
   c) To develop a database of schools, both primary and secondary, pupil populations, trained and untrained teachers in the South.

2. Teacher training courses to identify qualified persons to be trained of whom some could become trainers

of teachers on curriculum/syllabus, textbooks and teachers' guides.

3 Educational support to organise and distribute school materials, to plan for the rehabilitation of key schools in those areas with high school children in the South.

4 Curriculum management.
   a) To estimate and cost text books based on new curriculum for South Sudan;
   b) To facilitate curriculum development for lower and upper primary schools;
   c) To monitor trials of text books based on the new syllabus;
   d) To set up an examination board for the South; and
   e) To identify areas of new curriculum not competently taught so as to establish in-service course(s) training.

I was very enthusiastic to contribute positively to citizens of the South. Forced out from the college of education where I had resolved to make my capability available under hard conditions as explored in Chapter Six. There were the same challenges of education in the NSCC. An estimation of the number of new text books on the new curriculum was costed and presented to the chairman of SPLM/A to find funds. His simple statement after examining figures of six digits was that it would be considered as our financial situation improved but war was of greater concern.

The "motto" of the SPLM was to fight the Sudan government as well as pay attention to development. Normal activities were conducted at SPLM/A liberated areas. Seminars and conferences were held in the towns of Maridi, Yambio, Mapel,

Rumbek and other places. Small planes transported conferees to the South at risk from both Ugandan rebels of the Lord's Resistance Army, LRA and Sudan armed forces.

One morning, we flew out of Lokichoggio airport to the South. It was very cloudy and the pilot flew in the thick clouds to the small town of Ikatos in Eastern Equatoria to pick up a person to attend a conference in Nimule. The pilot, apprehensive of anti-LRA aircraft, trusted himself and his plane and flew into rain-bearing clouds. However, we landed safely on Nimule airstrip. That was an example of how often we were exposed to danger in order to attend so many functions held in liberated towns.

Rehabilitation and activation of key schools was on my table of action. Among so many schools to be rehabilitated and activated was the old, famous and prestigious Rumbek Secondary School. An articulated programme for renovation of the school was written and presented to a Catholic NGO in Nairobi responsible for such programmes in the South. The project was costed at US$150,000 which was rejected by my boss of the education department in that the project couldn't be sponsored by the Catholic NGO. It was too costly, she told me.

Patiently I explained that it had to be tried. It wouldn't take time on my side to write a covering letter on the project to the NGO, signed by her. Reluctantly she signed the letter and I made sure the letter was dispatched as I had grounds to suspect her.

After a month I heard in international news one morning that the Sudan Desk in Washington DC was going to sponsor maintenance of RSSS. A concerned lady was to take the cheque of US$150,000 to Rumbek. The announcement excited me and what stimulated it came in international news. I heard the news while I was in Yambio town, Western Equatoria, where I attending a workshop on education sponsored by Unicef.

Her contemptuous attitude to all that I did in the department was proved by her behaviour when I informed her about the sponsorship by the Sudan Desk in Washington. She was very negative, which surprised me. The success of the education desk would go to her as the boss. It became abundantly clear to me that whatever I did was not going to be appreciated by her. I made the decision to continue doing what was within my capacity because the South would benefit.

My presence in the department was a threat to her position as the head. She felt one day I would replace her, which she didn't like at all. She reported to the executive secretary of NSCC that I was redundant and should be relieved of my duties. A friend tipped me off that a conspiracy was to be hatched. I listed all conferences attended in the South and Nairobi and gave reports of my activities in the department, including programmes written to rehabilitate and activate schools that had been successfully implemented. All that was presented to the executive secretary, who never talked to me about it. I expected him to call me for further inquiries and I waited patiently.

The executive secretary became aware of my boss' intentions towards me. The executive secretary knew very well my hard work and positive attitude back in Sudan before he went to study in the United States. I headed the department of planning in the Regional Ministry of Education and everybody going for further studies had their application passed to my desk for recommendation.

I realised that almost all the senior staff including the executive secretary of NSCC hadn't worked in an institution before. They lacked the attitude of teamwork that exists in any organisation. I further discovered that every morning after signing up for the day's attendance, each would go and greet the executive secretary, a routine that became an office activity. It was a puzzle what would be told to him every morning as it seemed a group misinformed, especially my boss, who behaved like an informer, a Kenyan intelligence agent planted in the organisation.

Her behaviour didn't bother me, for I performed my duties to the best of my ability as expected of me. I didn't look to her position and as a refugee was content with my salary to pay for shelter and subsistence.

The worst action she did was to break a drawer of my table to remove documents. One of the documents was an outline of a topic I wanted to write on. I almost lost my temper to the point of awarding her an open hand slap to send her down on floor. Something within me shouted "Stop! Wait!" as I stood in front of her table I shook with anger, then slowly I walked to my office. I sat silently at my table for a complete 15 minutes without talking. Those sharing the cubical office with me asked if something was wrong and I answered negatively, but they knew it must be between me and my boss.

The voice of reason shouted within my mind to avoid violence. Later on when I had cooled down I praised my behaviour. I could have ended up in a prison and blamed. Nobody would justify my violence, no matter what. Instead, my children would suffer more than me and end up in Kakuma, the biggest refugee camp in north-western Kenya. However, she utterly failed to remove me, but was always on the lookout for any slim opportunity to push me off a cliff.

The opportunity came at last. I became very mobile between Kampala, Nairobi and liberated towns in the South. The sub office of education transferred to Kampala. I travelled to Pageri, Nimule and other villages in the vicinity. I stayed for about ten days and became sick when I arrived in Nairobi which meant I was hospitalised for two days. When I was discharged I left for Kampala, as it was better to be with family. I reported to my family a doctor and the two Indian brothers recommended I be admitted to Nzambya hospital in Kampala in September 2002. The hospital educated citizens with diabetes on diet, self-injection with insulin and general management of the condition.

A small wound developed on the tip of the big toe of my right foot. The whole leg was swollen and doctors argued whether to amputate my leg below the knee. Dr Otim, a professor of medicine in the University of Makerere, led the argument that if the whole leg was removed I would die. Unconscious and unable to talk, my opinion couldn't be sought and my dear wife opposed the amputation option. The opposition of my devoted wife and Dr Otim won the day. The other doctors feared gangrene would affect the whole leg and result in death.

The toe was amputated. The nurses became careless with the wound and it became septic. The situation deteriorated and I didn't know myself, let alone relatives who came to see me. Dr Otim took over my treatment and transferred me to Kololo hospital where he worked. I struggled with life with my dedicated wife at my bedside. Dr Otim never gave up, changing from drug to drug.

One, day life almost left me. I was on a drip with four medicines being administered intravenously into my blood system, when the drip stopped. My heart (the central pumping system) was at a point of stopping beating. My doctor told my wife that the whole case was left to God. All my children went to the hospital to witness what would be a big event that would change their lives for worse. However, my wife and daughters were very brave and waited for the time my soul would leave my body. The doctor did what he could to prevent what was inevitable, but the final action was with God and unbelievably the drip started very slowly to flow into my blood system again. The doctor, the nurses, my wife and daughters looked at each other uncertainly. Life came back to me and the movement of the drip in the tube was a sure sign that my heartbeat was back to normality. The drama of dreadful magnitude ended wonderfully and peacefully.

Days after that terrifying experience, I was discharged to continue treatment and recuperate in my residence in Kampala. The hospital bills had skyrocketed in a country where Medicare did not exist. My elder son Takpiny Marial Takpiny, a student-refugee in Canada, contributed to settle the bill. My two cousins, the late Dr Parmena Marial Akuocpiir Malual and Mr John Buong Dhieu Malual, presented a rescue fund. Other relatives and friends donated generously, among them Professor Moses Macar Kacuol, my brother-in-law, the late Mr Winston Magong Simon Ngong, Dr Akech koch, who is married to one of my sisters in law, Mabuto Simon Ngong, another brother-in-law, sister in law, Ajok Simon Ngong and others. That was the bill paid.

My colleagues of NSCC offered financial and moral support under the leadership of the late Gabriel Mayor Makuei. They paid frequent hospital visits and prayed at my bedside. All friends and acquaintances including non-Sudanese visitors came to the hospital.

What happened during my sickness before I could come to school was the talk and concern of the people of Parial Gok village and the whole of Ajak and Kuac. The same occurred in 2002, when relatives and friends became concerned in Australia, USA, Canada, United Kingdom and other European countries. The appreciation of welfare wishers from relatives, friends and acquaintances wouldn't be complete without mentioning the visit of our late leader Dr John Garang de Mabior Atem. He came to see me in my residence with his security men, headed by commander Gier Chuang Aluong. At that time, I was a talking skeleton that couldn't walk.

He contributed very much to my journey to Australia. I made it clear to him that I had two objectives to leave the movement still had not accomplished its mission: to seek further treatment and to get my children to pursue education. The two goals sounded convincing and commendable to him.

An opportunity came to my opponent in the NSCC. The head of the education department again raised a memorandum for me to be relieved of my activities in the organisation. The leadership didn't know how to deal with such a delicate matter and above all her word seemed not to be questioned critically.

Before my complete convalescence I received a notification that my employment with the organisation was terminated. Being in that fragile position physically and mentally, I could have fallen dead receiving that discouraging and demoralising information. Perhaps my background training in counselling did help me.

My eyesight became weak. An eye specialist told me that a cataract had developed in the left eye. I thought that since I had filled a form for resettlement that an operation could be conducted in a country of resettlement.

The termination of my services in the NSCC confronted me with three problems: no job, no funds for rent and my daughters not in school. The alternative was to move to a refugee camp.

The three issues compelled me to consider and I accepted to search for a country to take me for resettlement. I had resisted the idea of going for resettlement earlier on. With my health condition and no education for my daughters who were assets, we filled in a form for resettlement. The form was accepted and so began a long process. It went well except it was complicated by a lady who was desperate for bribery in the International Organisation for Migration, IOM Uganda office. She was determined to extract dollars out of poor refugees going on resettlement. She became rich at the expense of refugees and destroyed the chances of those refugees unable to pay her.

The author's father, Takpiny Malual Apar, Yirol paramount chief on his compound in Parial Village in 1934

Alede Manyang Agok, the author's mother, at the Commissioner's residence in Rumbek town, 1980

The author, Professor Martin Marial Takpiny and his wife, Mrs Susan Ajak Simon Ngong

The author's son, Mr Takpiny Marial Takpiny

Mrs Deer Marial Takpiny and her husband, Mr Malang Kuanyin Bol with their daughter (author's granddaughter), Athiei Malang Kuanyin Bol.

Miss Adol Marial Takpiny

Miss Atong Marial Takpiny

Miss Ajok Marial Takpiny

Miss Adut Marial Takpiny

Mrs Alede Marial Takpiny and her husband, Mr Isaac Gatt

Chapter Eight

Immigration to the Land of the Kangaroo

Australia, the smallest continent in the world. It is a home to the kangaroo, an animal with strong, long hind legs. It leaps as it walks or runs and swims normally like other animals. It is native to Australia and New Guinea and is a big tourist attraction. It is the national emblem of Australia. Kangaroo belongs to the group of mammals that are known as marsupials, of which the females have a pouch that contains teats where the young are fed and carried (cited from a dictionary).

In Uganda the resettlement process was very elaborate. A complex medical examination took almost four or more months until we forgot the whole exercise. Fortunately, a notice of acceptance came to us and we were asked to report to the office. My children and their mother were excited. It was what they had looked forward to. Their wish was fulfilled and we waited impatiently for a day to depart.

We received directives to leave for Australia on 23 February 2004 and our residence was full of commotion and merriment from the children. They were to go to a continent they had read about only in geography books. The affirmation aroused a great enthusiasm in them.

The journey out of our residence in Wau in 1997 was not the same as that of Uganda 2004. We did not know what was ahead. The journey out of Wau was full of risks and we were not sure of a family reunion when we divided into two.

En route to Australia was very different from that of Wau where we went straight to the bushes of Southern Sudan. Australia was first world and we would get what we deserved accordingly. The joy of my children was fully justified, in anticipation of seeing their relatives and friends who used to communicate with us during our long wait in Uganda.

At 3:00 am we arrived at the IOM. There were other refugees also en route to Australia. By 5:00 am we were in Entebbe airport and took off for Nairobi, Kenya. Upon our arrival we saw somebody standing with a small board and written on it, the word "refugees". He led us to an international transit lounge and showed us the convenience unit.

After about one hour at Jomo Kenyatta International Airport we boarded a South Africa Airline plane. My eyesight was so poor I couldn't see the countryside, especially at landing. We landed in Johannesburg, South Africa. The country became known all over the world for the wrong reason: apartheid, the policy of racial segregation that was in place before the African National Congress, ANC, government of reconciliation led by President Nelson Mandela.

The reception we received at Nairobi Airport was not the same in Johannesburg. The refugees were at a complete loss. They moved here and there to locate where to sit and waited. Somebody took it upon himself to discover the right place to wait. After half an hour staying there an aggressive, quarrelsome lady arrived at the desk. The refugees to Sydney,

Australia, neatly lined up. The lady started an argument and blamed everybody until she ended what she was doing with the refugees.

The behaviour of the lady could be justified in terms of an apartheid era where non-white South Africans were not allowed to handle such jobs. She had to adjust to being punctual, taking an appropriate approach to people and being emotionally self-controlled. Her behaviour didn't disturb me, but I took pity on her. Then she disappeared without telling the passengers anything. Without knowing what the next step was, we were thankful to be waiting in a comfortable lounge.

The day went quietly and we waited for our plane to arrive at about 6:00 pm local time. A huge plane pulled into the apron with the emblem of an animal on its tail. Looking at it more carefully, a picture of a kangaroo emerged and the plane was marked Qantas. It became known later that Qantas stands for Queensland and Northern Territory Aerial Services, now the Australian national carrier.

After boarding, the big machine gently and confidently coursed into the atmosphere to reach an altitude of about 34,000 feet above sea level, heading south-east from Jan Smuts Airport. The destination was Sydney airport without stopping. It took Qantas 14 hours flying over the ocean to reach Sydney airport in the afternoon.

I gave a sigh of relief to disembark the plane. My knees ached as my long legs couldn't fit under the seat. There was no option but to bear it, with little adjustments of my knees when it became unbearable. The flight was smooth all the way to Sydney. I couldn't see the outline of the great city because of my poor eyesight.

The passengers who were refugees were directed to different desks at exits, either transit or destination Sydney.

Members of my family processed everything while I sat on a bench, a little bit sick. Clearance took a short while to finish and we walked out. Airport security clearances were not bothersome because their purpose is to stop those who kill innocent people "in the name of God" or drug traffickers and other contraband stuffs.

A group of our relatives and friends waited like a task force. An atmosphere of happiness and excitement prevailed. We hadn't seen each other for more than a decade and we discovered some friends who we thought we had lost track of. This was a reunion engulfed by jubilation.

Antipas Apaak Kot, James Majok Ater, the late John Gum Lang and others gave us the warmest reception on Australian soil. It was like a dream from the suburb of Kampala city. The dream became true to all of us in the family. The journey that began in the afternoon of Wednesday 20 May 1997 ended successfully after seven years in 2004. We never anticipated being on another continent in high spirits when we departed Wau in a sad and downcast mood.

The team headed to the residence of Antipas Apaak at a suburb of Sydney city, and more persons in the residence welcomed us to a new and vibrant life in Australia. We were at home and thankful to Antipas Apaak and James Majok, who did everything to ensure our coming to the land of the kangaroo. They mobilised the Yirol community in Sydney to make our travel possible and easy.

We finished our first meal and Antipas Apaak led us to the compound of the Church of Christ where accommodation was arranged. Our first residence in Australia was fully furnished with a big refrigerator packed with a week's supply of food by Antipas Apaak with his wife, Monica Rool Dhieu Malual, my niece. There could be no better accommodation than the one prepared by a dedicated person like Antipas Apaak.

The Australian government under the Federal Ministry of Immigration came to an understanding with the churches and other organisations to receive and accommodate immigrants until they could settle on their own with some assistance from the local community. The immigrants get their basic needs, utensils, beds, blankets and furniture, including a family size refrigerator.

The immigrants are introduced to a general practitioner, GP near the location of their accommodation, the Medicare office to get a card (Medicare) which is a must and important, Centrelink- a federal government office that deals with welfare matters- and a bank. The GP gives medical services and Centrelink provides financial necessities, a lot of orientation is given to immigrants, including operation of an automatic teller machine, ATM to get cash.

The immigrants were de-traumatised in order to feel and be normal and only tackle cultural shock as they have landed into a foreign culture. The background of many immigrants associated with violence, repressive regimes and humiliation, submerged into a stream of freedom and recognition as a fellow human being. A good number of them wondered and were confused, especially when everybody possessed a bank account, a situation never experienced where they came from.

Educationally, my children benefited from East Africa because they came with a background in which English language had been a medium of instruction in school previously from educational institutions such as the Catholic school of St Francis in Khartoum. They had no difficulties in the Ugandan system with the English language. They adapted quickly to the Australian system at different levels of education.

However, we began to realise our objectives that drove us into immigration in Australia. My daughters' thirst for education from East Africa, where lack of funds prevented them proceeding with further education, grabbed their chance. The education had they received in East Africa prepared them for further education.

It is to be mentioned at this junction that the Australian system is geared to employment. As a child approaches Year 12 they formulate what to do with their life with the help of an academic counsellor. After Year 12 many children would prefer to be admitted to TAFE where skills taught enable them to graduate with a diploma. The skills acquired at TAFE generally guarantee a job in the Australian markets of employment. After obtaining a job a graduate could seek admission to university and the TAFE diploma may be considered as credits towards the university course. This system allows a student to work and study. Double degrees are becoming more popular in the Australian system of higher education to widen a student's chances in the employment market. Hence, my daughters could easily get a job with one of the degrees. The system guarantees jobs for graduates but not education for the sake of it.

Four of my daughters were admitted to universities. Miss Ajok Marial Takpiny graduated with a bachelor of nursing as a registered nurse from the University of Technology Sydney in 2008. Her sister, Miss Alede Marial Takpiny, followed in the footsteps of Ajok and graduated with a bachelor of nursing as a registered nurse in 2009, and in 2012 she graduated with her second degree in midwifery, both from the University of Western Sydney. Miss Adol Marial Takpiny was admitted to the University of Western Sydney to graduate with a double degree, bachelor of communications studies/Bachelor of Law.

Miss Adut Marial Takpiny graduated with a triple degree of bachelor of international studies, bachelor of public relations and bachelor of communications from the University of Canberra (the capital of Australia).

The youngest member of the family, Miss Atong Marial Takpiny, was admitted to the University of Technology Sydney where she is currently studying for a Bachelor of Design in Fashion and Textiles. Miss Deer Marial Takpiny was awarded a diploma in hospitality from the Institute of Hospitality, involving the management of hotels and associated businesses.

The mother of the family, my dear wife Mrs Susan Ajak Simon Ngong, studied English as a preparation for vocational training. All members of the family were involved in education to enter the Australian system of the labour force, to enable them to be easily employed. I am proud to say all of my daughters have worked and studied part time to earn bread for our family.

Miss Deer Marial Takpiny completed her studies and moved back to South Sudan for work, then married Mr Malang Kuanyin Bol on 14 July 2011. In December 2013 I became the proud grandfather of Deer's first daughter, Athiei Malang Kuanyin. Miss Adol Marial Takpiny has worked for the Australian government for many years and her current role is project coordinator with the Department of Justice. After Miss Adut Marial Takpiny graduated she also relocated back to South Sudan to work and pursue further studies. Miss Ajok Marial Takpiny worked in the Australian public health system for several years and is now working as an expert at King Faisal Specialist and Research Centre, Riyadh, Saudi Arabia. Miss Alede Marial Takpiny has also been working in the Australian public health system for several years as both a registered nurse and registered midwife. She was married on 14

April 2012 to Mr Isaac Paul Gatt. Miss Atong Marial Takpiny has been working with a renowned Australian designer Carl Zampatti as part of her internship programme.

As mentioned elsewhere in the book, I was concerned about my health. The sickness which hospitalised me in Kampala left me in a state of weakness. No sooner had I arrived in Sydney than I was directed to an appropriate health centre.

To make an appointment in a hospital with a specialist takes months and at times a year. The first appointment was in a big hospital, Westmead University Clinics, the biggest hospital in the southern hemisphere. It can best be described as a three-dimensional shape: horizontal, vertical and downward. At the main entrance a four wheeled electric machine is driven (by a driver) to deliver a patient/an elderly person to further away elevators.

The first appointment was my first encounter with a dietician with different types of foodstuffs around to illustrate points of explanation. In Africa my diet consisted mainly of foods high in proteins and very little carbohydrates. Rice was forbidden to eat under the direction of dieticians there. The dietician introduced me to all foods with emphasis on vegetables and fruits. If carbohydrates were avoided, how would one get energy for all that is to be done, including thinking?

The specialist on diabetes stopped administration of insulin to me. I injected myself before breakfast with insulin overseas, but the specialist prescribed three drugs instead of insulin. My condition was classified as diabetes type two or the mellitus common type, to be controlled with tablets, so that was good news. The glucose blood level was to be monitored before every meal. Within three months the diabetes was controlled and blood analysis after every three months to monitor the usual victims of kidneys and eyes showed they were coping with the diabetes. Three monthly blood analysis also helps to detect the malfunction of other organs or uncover latent infection and "nip it in the bud".

It was discovered in Uganda that cataracts had developed in my eyes and a Sydney eye hospital treated my eye ailments. Nevertheless, there's a real alarm in the left eye. The senior eye specialist informed me of a blood clot in one of the veins of the retina whose nerves are responsible for formation of images, my sight. He explained that my eye needed to be stimulated so that my body could remove the clot and if not a physical operation would have to be performed. He warned me that I could lose my sight. That was frightening.

The eye was stimulated and the body refused to act. The dangerous but inevitable option of an operation remained. The clot would generate further complications in the eye and to remove it would either give the success of normal sight or loss of it. The situation in the Uganda hospital was repeated, whether to amputate the big toe or the whole leg. My dedicated wife made the decision on my behalf. The choice was left to me whether to remove the clot manually and my answer was affirmative. The operation was carried out one afternoon and the following morning an examination indicated loss of sight in the eye. Other medical procedures were conducted on the eye to let the eyeball remain its normal shape without vision and not sink into the eye socket. The equation seemed completed: no vision in the left eye and no big toe on the right foot.

The diabetes took its toll on me. I lost a big toe in the Ugandan hospital and as a result I arrived in Australia with nine toes. In June 2004 I became a one eyed person, losing sight in the left eye. Needless to say, a war has been going on between me and the diabetes and what happened were consequences of the clash. Therefore, my GP was on the lookout not to let confrontation, occur again. My GP was doing something like what the UN does among the belligerent nations to avoid a Third World War.

I stayed one year in Australia and became a senior citizen. I reached the age of pension at 65 years old in 2005, which is now raised to 67 years. I am now 75 years old (2016). Australia is an ageing continent with ever increasing numbers of elderly people. These elders are given the respectable name of seniors. They are given special treatment to possess a concession card for reduced fare tickets of public transport both in buses and trains. Similarly, with pharmacies, drugs are sold at half the price to them. The seniors enjoy many more privileges.

On 31 August 2006, I was born again. I became an Australian citizen to benefit from all aspects of life on the continent. I and three members of my family were awarded certificates of citizenships together with a seedling. I philosophised that the seedling was a symbol to grow and be productive. We were to fulfil the story in the Bible which says that some seeds fell on a rock, others on infertile soil and the rest on fertile ground. The seeds on the fertile soil grew into healthy plants that blossomed and produced healthy crops. It's speculated that this is a continent where one could successfully develop capabilities for self-betterment and the country as a whole.

The seedling symbol was fulfilled. The family is blossoming despite my dear wife becoming ill from a stroke. My intelligent daughters were admitted to institutions of higher learning and are now in the Australian workforce. Their employment was processed immediately because of the acute need for skilled workers in the country.

The family ran into difficulties when the mother of the family became sick. I was devastated when she was admitted to Westmead Hospital in Sydney. She was struck by stroke. In common language, a stroke is the interruption of the flow of blood into the brain, disabling functioning of some parts of a person's body. In her case, the right part of her body was slightly weak. God was with us all along.

It occurred on 4 June 2007. She spent one month in Westmead Hospital and then transferred to St Joseph's Hospital, also in Sydney, which specialised in management of stroke patients. She spent another month under all types of therapies. The therapies take a long time to bring a patient to normalcy. Other therapies were carried out in nearby hospitals or at our residence.

The stroke slowed the mother of the family in her growth as expected in Australia. However, she fully recovered and we thank God.

It is our wish and hope that the whole family blossom as expected on the continent of opportunities, the land of the kangaroo.

Epilogue

My late uncle Dhieu Malual Apar was a reformer who was blamed when he took me to school. Some people in the area talked openly that Dhieu Malual did that to keep the son of his brother away from taking chieftainship from him because chieftainship is inherited. It was believed that I would inherit it when grown to an age yet that wasn't my thinking at all.

It is to be mentioned that my mother Alede Manyang Agok was another reformer at that time when education was not valued. Had she rejected my school attendance, this book wouldn't be in your hands now. She became enlightened during the short periods she accompanied her husband Takpiny to Yirol during tribal disputes settlement. She knew that education was worth doing and consented for me to go to school. It seems that my father Takpiny Malual wouldn't take me to school. He died before I could become of school age. He would have liked to keep me out of school to be a keeper of his numerous herds of cattle.

I was to disprove the belief at that time that education spoiled children. Tonj Primary School proved it wrong. The Apar family became educated. Many children attended school after me and I am happy that I am an example. It is my wish that a good number of children get a better education than me. I would claim without a doubt that I am a father of education in the Ajak section. The parents admired what I did and sent their children to school.

The rural population is still depending on subsistence livelihood. No commercial agriculture developed in the whole South Sudan despite the fact that the area has wonderful potential for agriculture. The agricultural development is a big challenge to the government of the country.

The livestock remains without improvement as I was deprived of cattle keeping about half a century ago. Although cattle are kept for livelihood by the Dinka, there have been no improvements made on cattle to produce both quality and quantity of milk and meat, let alone development of other cattle products. The cattle have been responsible for the complacency of the Dinka life led since they appeared on the planet.

It is appropriate to comment on "complacency" as mentioned in Chapter Two of this book, where a brief account is given on the activities of citizens of Parial Gok. Complacency means to be uncritically contented with what you have or with your life, with no efforts made to change life for the better.

Complacency has been brought about by a cow in Dinka life. The cow brings milk in the morning and evening and there is contentment to that way of life. All activities are connected to the cow and there was a culture of the cow, whereby people are dependent on the cow. As such, many pleasures and disputes centre on the cow.

It is safe to say that complacency makes people lazy, unproductive and uncreative, and consequently poor. The complacency transfers to working government employees in towns and this is what is happening to the Dinka, whereby the people working for paid jobs provide for the needs of relatives crowded in their residences. The dependants don't want to work since their basic needs are fulfilled by the working officials.

How does an individual improve financially, if dependency on cattle is transferred to him or her? There is a migration trend to the towns and the working officials are to accommodate the migrants. It seems the Nilotic working officials have a social problem to be handled with care.

For instance, Mr Q Public is a working official accommodating Mr Wut, who has been visited by Mr Kuat. Mr Raneben has come to Mr Kuat seeking medical treatment. The three persons in the residence of Mr Q Public are Mr Wut, the first guest, Mr Kuat, the second guest and Mr Raneben with his wife as the third guest. They would be referred to as guest of guest of guest of the guest. It forms a melody in Dinka as Kaman, Kaman, Kaman.

Mr Q Public can't do anything except to bear it, although ends could not meet in his household. The culture encourages such a state of affairs. Mr Q Public couldn't chase them away from his residence for fear that "negative sayings and songs" could be composed and publicised against him.

What is to be done to that significant percentage of the population in the towns and rural areas doing no productive activities for themselves or the whole community at large? Dependency and complacency have become social ills to be got rid of in the community. The dependents and loafers are able bodies who can work. With the help of those concerned, the social workers can free the community from these social ills. This could be worked out to be a part of a general scheme of development in the republic.

The Republic of South Sudan needs to initiate very aggressive and vigorous programmes of development towards modernity to include issues such as dependency, complacency and redundancy which tend to retard progress. The priorities to facilitate advancement are envisioned as follows:

Security
Without it no development would take place as has been sufficiently shown during 39 years of struggle with Sudan's ruling class. Any little progress before 2005 is the result of ten years of tranquillity in the South from 1972 to 1982. The North made the South ungovernable during that period to show the world that the South couldn't govern itself. During the six years, the contrary has been proved right.

Law and order
Security goes together with law and order. Law and order was extremely relaxed in the South during the interim period from 2006 to 2011 due to the referendum. The NCP took advantage of the situation to arm those Nilotic peoples whose cattle had been raided. There had been raids and counter raids with many lives lost. A high level of law and order needed to be maintained after the birth of a new nation on 9 July 2011.

Agriculture
It is a necessity to have food security all the time. There is plenty of arable land throughout the republic should there need to be a law formulated to force malingerers to work to be independent. The law needs to include dependents who have one common thing, complacency, which breeds poverty.

Education
Seven decades of education made the South become the Republic of South Sudan. Education is the key to self-improvement, development and modernity. It's the function of

progress. The town malingerers and indolent rural people need to be targeted for adult education to allow them to participate in the development of the republic of the South Sudan.

Transport and roads
Network tarmac roads make mobility of commodities, goods and people easy and quick. For instance, refrigerated trucks could bring tropical fruits from there to other parts of the country.

Health
Proper identification of common diseases, control and distribution of medicines and drugs, the population to be healthy and actively participate in this development, and parallel with human health is animal welfare. The lives of livestock and other domestic animals need to be improved to provide better meat, milk and other products from the animals.

The six components of development outlined above need to be short and long term projects and be executed in letter and spirit. Every project needs to be time-sensitive which means each finishes on schedule. The programmes need to be forcefully implemented. The dependants, the malingerers and idlers must benefit financially from the projects.

The overall goal is to make the population of the Republic of South Sudan secure, law abiding, reducing or eliminating illiteracy, so they have food security, network tarmac roads, are healthy and have a developed culture of hard work and above all self-dependency. This could be called the roadmap to modernise the young Republic of South Sudan.

It is in the field of education where a pronounced progress is noted. The educated class running the South are the seven decades of education in the South, especially the Dinka who previously resisted education. The dispersal of Dinka as refugees in different countries was seen as a curse but has become a blessing education-wise. For instance, my four daughters graduated from universities which might not have happened if we had remained in East Africa or in Sudan. However, education needs to accelerate its spread in South Sudan and further with the diaspora.

The political discontent made the people of former Southern Sudan take up arms again. The circumstances forced me out of Wau town and I wanted to take cover in the villages, which couldn't work. During my move southwards from Wau town, I wore different hats: the hat of an IDP in Mapuordit village in the South, the refugee hat in East Africa and immigrant hat in the land of the kangaroo, Australia. I became a dual citizen, of the Republic of South Sudan and Australia.

References

Arop, Arop Madut, *Sudan's Painful Road to Peace*, page 187, Book Surge LLC 2006

Ulrich, Karen, *How To Write Your Life Story: The Complete Guide to Creating Personal Memoir*, The Reader's Digest Association, Inc., Pleasantville, New York, Ivy Press Limited, 2006

Acknowledgements

In writing this booklet, I received support from several people. I owe a debt of gratitude to them.

I give an unreserved and full recognition to my son-in-law, **Isaac Gatt**, who typed the script of this book from hard-to-read handwritten material. He laboured tirelessly to complete the script. At times one feels it is insufficient to simply say Thank you for great work done.

While I was scribbling the notes that became the ingredients of the book, my wife, **Susan Ajak** and all of our daughters were giving me their full support. The family created an atmosphere conducive to writing within the house and knew when to serve me with tea or drinking water when they knew I needed a break and refreshment.

Editors **Cheryl Bettridge** and **Catherine Schwerin** have done a great job in ridding the text of some expressions and phrases that were obscure. They also deserve praise for dealing with several abbreviations and acronyms that are South Sudanese-specific. That this book is readable is partly due to their efforts to improve the draft to make the story flow smooth and better.

I am grateful to **Dut A. Y. Atem** and his design company for producing the illustration for the cover that is gracing the book. His drawing is worth more than a thousand words, to borrow a cliché.

Peter Lual Reech Deng, the CEO of the Africa World Books, and his colleague, **Manyang Deng Biar,** have played an important part in making the story of my life appear between two covers. From the first contact with me, and without hesitation, Peter did not only accept to have the book published; he assured me that the mission of the African World Books is to promote writings, fiction or non-fiction, by South Sudanese at home or in the diaspora. The African World Books and its pioneering and young entrepreneurs deserve both my gratitude and encouragement for the good work they are doing: promoting the documentation by non-export members of the public- the past and present of South Sudan.

Finally, I sincerely acknowledge all the persons – including those persons I might have inadvertently forgotten – for their contributions to this work in one way or another. While I am grateful to all of them, they at the same time have no part in the book's shortcomings or in the opinions and interpretations of the events described in this autobiography. I take full responsibility for them as the author of this modest work.

www.ingramcontent.com/pod-product-compliance
Lightning Source LLC
Chambersburg PA
CBHW020620300426
44113CB00007B/720